GUANO STAINS GRANDMA

aka

Astounding Anagrams

ROBOT SHOCKS ITALIAN

ISBN 1 85868 885 X

A CIP Catalogue for this book is available from the British Library

Executive Editor: Mould Deposit
Senior Art Editor: Brow Mint
Design: Jeers Hail Chic Usages
Production: Harm To Barber

Printed and bound in England

The authors would like to thank Tim Dedopulos (Doomed Tulips); Claire Forker (Rare rock life); Mr Peter Bannon (Bent prominent ears); Mister Brendan Bannon (An inbred snob remnant); Dan Southwell (Hallowed nuts); Sean Twist (Wet stains); Sean York (Yak snore); Leigh Tomkins (OK slime thing); David Brooks (Sir Vodka Bod); Simon Dove (Vein moods) Orlando Plunket Green (Elegant round plonker) and a host of other folk including Ed; Debbie; Syvel; Francis; Steve; Chris; Mike and David Smith.

GUANO STAINS GRANDMA

aka

Astounding Anagrams

David Southwell and Anne-Marie Forker

CARLTON

☆ CONTENTS ☆

20TH CENTURY AUTHORS

Morris West	*Worst miser*
Leslie Marmon Silko	*Loser makes million*
Carol Shields	*Scholar idles*
Irving Wallace	*Crawling alive*
Ellen Gilchrist	*Still lechering*
Thomas Ligotti	*To limit a ghost*
Alastair Maclean	*I am a Satan caller*
Cleveland Amory	*My calendar love*
Douglas Copeland	*Loud gonadal cups*
Patrick O'Brien	*Baritone prick*
Anne McCaffrey	*Fancy farce men*
James Baldwin	*Main lewd jabs*
Charles Bukowski	*Housebricks walk*
Patricia Cornwall	*Now practical liar*
Anne Rice	*Acne rein*
Thomas Pynchon	*Not nympho cash*
Barbara Kingsolver	*Broken arrival bags*
Ishmael Reed	*Header smile*
Joseph Wambaugh	*Ha! Huge swamp job*
Eileen Groudge	*Need uglier ego*
Tom Robbins	*Snort bimbo*
Irving Stone	*Onset virgin*
Gloria Naylor	*Loony rag liar*
Alice Walker	*Wreak ill, ace*
Joyce Carol Oates	*A cool jersey coat*

BEST SELLING AUTHORS

Stephen King	*He's pink gent*
Virginia Andrews	*Arid raving swine*
Jackie Collins	*Clinical jokes*
Barbara Erskine	*Ask brain-bearer*
Patricia Scanlan	*Is carnal captain*
Dean Koontz	*On zonk date*
Catherine Cookson	*No! A shock erection*
Minette Walters	*Master new title*
Craig Thomas	*Got charisma*
Helen Fielding	*Define gin hell*
Thomas Harris	*Hash arms riot*
Kathy Reichs	*Hairy sketch*
Jilly Cooper	*Jolly copier*
Terry Brooks	*Story broker*
Wilbur Smith	*Hi! Bum twirls*
Patricia Cornwell	*Caterpillar in cow*
James Herbert	*Jeer them bras*
David Gemmel	*Mad devil gem*
John Grisham	*Horns jag him*
Danielle Steel	*Senile led tale*
Michael Crichton	*Chronic lame itch*
Len Deighton	*O! Thin legend*
Clive Egleton	*I neglect love*
Robin Cook	*Oi! Rock nob*
Ted Allbeury	*Ready bullet*

BRITISH 20TH CENTURY AUTHORS

Irvine Welsh	*His new liver*
Salman Rushdie	*Smashed urinal*
Clive Barker	*Blacker river*
Barbara Taylor Bradford	*Dartboard far-away blob*
Anita Brookner	*Karate on Robin*
Colin Dexter	*Old ex-cretin*
John Kilian Brunner	*Na! Horrible junk inn*
Antonio Byatt	*A batty notion*
Barbara Cartland	*A drab carnal brat*
Arthur Clarke	*A chart lurker*
Bernard Cornwell	*Rarer clown blend*
Daphne du Maurier	*Dream up nude hair*
Ian Fleming	*Failing men*
Frederick Forsyth	*Freed frisky torch*
Stephen Hawking	*A knight's nephew*
Georgette Heyer	*He regret ego yet*
Michael Korda	*I'm a older hack*
David John Lodge	*Old dog hand jive*
Alan Garner	*Gnarl arena*
Anne Perry	*Rare penny*
Mary Stewart	*Yes! Warm tart*
Rosemary Sutcliff	*Foul, merry fascist*
Susan Townsend	*Now sadness nut*
Joanna Trollope	*Polar jet on loan*
Fay Weldon	*A downy elf*

BRITISH COMEDIANS OF THE 1960S AND 1970S

Eric Morecambe	*Mere comic bear*
Ernie Wise	*Rise in ewe*
Tony Hancock	*Conch to Yank*
Spike Milligan	*I kill mean pigs*
Terry Jones	*No! Try jeers*
Eric Sykes	*Yes, sicker!*
Graham Chapman	*Hmm! A pagan arch*
Phil Silvers	*Lip shrivels*
Jonathan Miller	*Hell! Join mantra*
Eric Idle	*Dire lice*
Michael Palin	*I'm plain leach*
Eleanor Bron	*Na! Loner bore*
William Rushton	*I worst ill human*
Bill Oddie	*Led libido*
Alfie Bass	*Fib ale ass*
Frankie Howard	*Oh! Inward freak*
Wilfred Brambell	*Warm dribble fell*
Harry H. Corbett	*Hot cherry brat*
Ronnie Barker	*In broken rear*
Gunner Beaumont	*Burn mean tongue*
Wilfred Hyde White	*Hey! Wed weird filth*
Terry Thomas	*My tart horse*
Alf Garnett	*Fart tangle*
Ronnie Corbett	*I born erect, not!*
Bill Fraser	*Bars' filler*

BRITISH COMEDIANS OF THE 1980S AND 1990S

Jasper Carrott	*Tart corpse jar*
Ben Elton	*Lent bone*
Russ Abbot	*A sob burst*
Dermot Morgan	*Drat! Gem moron*
Jennifer Saunders	*Darn! Jeers funnies*
Julian Clary	*A injury call*
Lilly Savage	*Ya! Evil slag!*
Steve Coogan	*Once vast ego*
Mel Smith	*Smelt him*
Ken Dodd	*No mean crap*
Dave Allen	*Anal delve*
Les Dawson	*Owns dales*
Kenny Everett	*Key rent event*
Paul Merton	*Manure plot*
Marti Caine	*I am a cretin*
Freddie Starr	*Farts derider*
Eddie Izard	*I ride dazed*
Mike Yarwood	*I moody wreck*
Bobby Davro	*By bravo bod*
Harry Enfield	*He randier fly*
Brian Conley	*Nicely baron*
Rowan Atkinson	*In on Satan work*
Reeves and Mortimer	*Over-rated miser men*
Victoria Wood	*Avoid cow riot*
Griff Rhys-Jones	*Grr! He sniffs joy!*

CHILDRENS AUTHORS

Enid Blyton	*Tiny blonde*
A.A Milne	*Am alien*
Michael Bond	*Him once bald*
Bonnie Bryant	*On brainy bent*
Beverly Cleary	*Very racy belle*
Richmal Crompton	*Imp-control charm*
Roald Dahl	*A hard doll*
Lucy Daniels	*A silly dunce*
Paula Danziger	*Pale Nazi guard*
Mary Norton	*Na! Try moron*
Nina Bawden	*I wanna bend*
Alan Gibbons	*Loan bin bags*
Michael Hardcastle	*Hell! Academic trash*
Dick King Smith	*Midnight kicks*
Clive King	*Given lick*
Sheila Lavelle	*Vile as hell ale*
Clive Staples Lewis	*Swap selective ills*
Ann Martin	*Mantra inn*
Brian Morse	*I'm rear snob*
Willard Price	*Ill weird crap*
Paul Shipton	*Ha! Pupil snot*
Angela Sommer Bodenburg	*Rambo's blue garden gnome*
Kaye Umansky	*May nuke a sky*
Susan Coolidge	*Uncle is good*
Leon Garfield	*Agile fondler*

CHILDRENS' BOOKS AND CHARACTERS

Harry Potter	*Try hero part*
Ramona The Pest	*Neat metaphors*
Christopher Robin	*Brother's iron chip*
My Name Is David	*My! Invade maids!*
The Mad Hatter	*Had tart theme*
What Katy Did	*Ha! Kiddy twat*
Charlotte's Web	*What erect slob*
Peter Pan	*Preen pat*
Paddington Bear	*Trained bad pong*
Winnie The Pooh	*I phone the wino*
Charlie And The Chocolate Factory	*Oh! Allocate a crotchety arch-fiend*
The Little Prince	*Help cretin title*
Little Red Riding Hood	*The drooling idle dirt*
The Adventures Of Tom Sawyer	*Nutty evades of whoremaster*
The Secret Garden	*Renegade Stretch*
Anne Of Avonlea	*A non-leaven oaf*
The House At Pooh Corner	*Ho ho! The snoop creature*
The Silver Chair	*Hitler archives*
The Winter Sleepwalker	*Knew all-white pesterer*
Anne Of Green Gables	*False gangrene bone*
The Railway Children	*Acid thrill anywhere*
Paddington At Large	*Departing natal God*
Five Get Into Trouble	*Refute violent bigot*
Timmy The Dog	*My dim ghetto*
Tales of a Fourth Grade Nothing	*Stuffed the arrogant hooligan*

CLASSIC NOVELISTS

Charles Dickens	*Clashed nickers*
Thomas Hardy	*Shy hot drama*
Stephen Crane	*Pest enhancer*
Louisa May Alcott	*Calamity to a soul*
Charlotte Bronte	*Once brothel tart*
Marcel Proust	*Creators lump*
Wilkie Collins	*Nice! I kill slow*
Joseph Conrad	*Jo chased porn*
Daniel Defoe	*Do feed alien!*
Alexandre Dumas	*Damn! Sexual dare*
Benjamin Disraeli	*Is in breadline jam*
William Faulkner	*Kill weariful man*
F. Scott Fitzgerald	*Glazed strict toff*
Emily Bronte	*To merely bin*
Ernest Hemmingway	*Whimsy meaner gent*
Thomas Hughes	*Oh, thug's shame*
Rudyard Kipling	*Aridly drunk pig*
D.H. Lawrence	*Drawn leech*
Thomas Mann	*Man shot man*
Sinclair Lewis	*Is arsenic will*
George Orwell	*Well, ogre gore*
John Steinback	*Ha! Inject knobs*
Robert Louis Stevenson	*Torn love-bite sourness*
Anthony Trollope	*He totally on porn*
Mark Twain	*Twin karma*

CLASSIC NOVELS

Pride and Prejudice	*Induce jaded ripper*
Sense and Sensibility	*Is tiny lesbian's needs*
The Woman In White	*With the mean wino*
Great Expectations	*Excite tart on pages*
The Last Of The Mohicans	*Ho ho! The mental fascist!*
Robinsoe Crusoe	*Obscure erosion*
Nicholas Nickelby	*Yank clinches boil*
Martin Chuzzlewit	*Mutant whizz relic*
David Copperfield	*Deprived acid flop*
A Tale Of Two Cities	*Ciao to latest wife*
Crime And Punishment	*Dinnertime chum naps*
Bleak House	*Oh! Elk abuse*
A Passage To India	*Against soap idea*
A Christmas Carol	*Scratch is amoral*
A Pair Of Blue Eyes	*Failures obey ape*
Far From The Madding Crowd	*God damn! Firm whored craft*
The Portrait Of A Lady	*Defy a harlot patriot*
The Turn Of The Screw	*Throw free chestnut*
The Half Sisters	*The selfish rats*
Lady Chatterley's Lover	*Cleverly steady harlot*
A Modern Lover	*Old rear venom*
Tom Sawyer And Huckleberry Fin	*Hey, demonstrably unfair wreck*
Around The World In Eighty Days	*Adultery showing dehadration*
Treasure Island	*Neural disaster*
Desperate Remedies	*Peer's steamier deed*

COMIC BOOK CHARACTERS

Desperate Dan	*Paraded teens*
The Punisher	*Hi psi-hunter*
The Invisible Woman	*Now I'm this enviable*
Superman	*Me sap urn*
The Amazing Spiderman	*Nightmares zap maiden*
The Incredible Hulk	*Be childlike hunter*
Captain America	*Practice a mania*
The Silver Surfer	*Sure filth-server*
Robin The Boy Wonder	*Oh! Weird rent-boy nob*
Denis The Menace	*I'm the dense acne*
Gnasher The Dog	*Gosh, the danger!*
Bash Street Kids	*Kit desserts? Bah!*
Wolverine	*Now eviler*
The Sub-Mariner	*Men are brutish*
Black Canary	*Cranky cabal*
Batman, the Caped Crusader	*Understated macabre chap*
The Joker	*O! The jerk*
Morpheus the Dreamlord	*Death rumpled her rooms*
Dare Devil	*Dread evil*
John Constantine	*John sat, innocent*
Doctor Strange	*God! Tart censor*
Phantom Stranger	*Ghost partner man*
The Flash	*Left hash*
The Shadow	*Hated show*
Swamp Thing	*Might spawn*

CRIME WRITERS

Dame Agatha Christie	*I am a right death case*
Natasha Cooper	*Aha! Not a corpse*
Robert Charles	*Brothels racer*
Colin Dexter	*Excel on dirt*
Carole Nelson Douglas	*Cool slanderous angel*
Margaret Erskine	*Sneakier rat germ*
Simon Shaw	*Smash wino*
George Goodchild	*Godchild ego ogre*
John Francome, author	*Oh no! major hunt farce*
John Grisham	*Shh! Groin jam*
Cynthia Harold Eagle	*Rallying to headache*
Charles Leader	*Sad career hell*
Bob Langley	*Angel lobby*
Roger Ormerod	*Groomed error*
Claire Rayner	*Alien rear cry*
Miss Ruth Rendell	*Hill's murder nest*
Joy Fielding	*Die, fling joy!*
Dorothy Simpson	*Not so dishy romp*
Peter Robinson	*Bones in report*
Martin Russell	*Terminal slurs*
Andrew Taylor	*A tawdry loner*
Rex Stout	*Sour text*
Peter Tremayne	*Enemy tart peer*
Arthur Upfield	*Laid further up*
Minette Walters	*Wettest mineral*

MODERN NOVELS

My Legendary Girlfriend	*Mildly fry dire gangrene*
Pearl In The Mist	*Sempiternal hit*
Head Over Heals	*Heroes have lad*
Nothing Lasts Forever	*Oh no! Self-serving tart*
Angels Of Mercy	*Clergyman's foe*
Altered State	*Deletes a tart*
She's Leaving Home	*Heavens! Hog slime*
The Heart Of London	*Oh no! Fondle threat!*
A Different Woman	*Endowment affair*
A Town Like Alice	*It woke Alliance*
A Dubious Legacy	*Usual acid bogey*
Constable In Control	*Not local cretin snob*
Friends And Relations	*Randiest infernal sod*
The Shadow Of Wings	*Done swift hogwash*
Everything To Gain	*I get tiny hangover*
Gentleman And Ladies	*Damndest alien angel*
The Accidental Tourist	*I castrated ethnic lout*
An Imaginative Experience	*I maniac teenager vixen pie*
An Indecent Obsession	*No! I insane second-best*
The Naked Face	*Fat dean cheek*
Key To The Door	*Oo! Hotter dyke*
The Final Cut	*That nice flu*
Bag Of Bones	*Safe bog nob*
Seize The Night	*High tit sneeze*
Point Of Origin	*Poof in rioting*

SCI-FI & FANTASY AUTHORS

Terry Pratchett	*Try pert chatter*
Ursula Le Guin	*Usual gin rule*
Michael Moorcock	*Calm comic hooker*
Terry Brooks	*Err...try books!*
Kim Stanley Robinson	*Am loony-bin stinkers*
William Gibson	*I'm wailing slob*
Piers Anthony	*Horny panties*
Stephen Baxter	*Has bent experts*
Arthur C. Clarke	*The rural cracker*
Michael Crichton	*Chromatic lichen*
Philip Jose Farmer	*Oh! Frail pimp jeers*
Harlan Ellison	*Aliens all horn*
Robert A. Heinlein	*Bent heroine liar*
Bruce Sterling	*Cretin rubs leg*
Marion Zimmer Bradley	*My bizarre mild moaner*
Orson Scott Card	*Sod contractors*
Stephen R. Donaldson	*Handles stoned porn*
Allan Dean Foster	*Fondle real Satan*
Neil Gaiman	*I'm alien nag*
Robert E Howard	*Drat! Whore bore*
Robert Rankin	*Terror in bank*
Storm Constantine	*No intact monsters*
Arthur Conan Doyle	*Annoy crude harlot*
Stanislaw Lem	*Well... Satanism*
Robert Jordan	*And terror job*
Kim Newman	*Men ink maw*

ACTION FILMS OF THE 1960S AND 1970S

Africa: Texas Style	*Tax-free catalysis*
Avalanche	*Naval ache*
Assault On A Queen	*Equal snot nausea*
Atlantis, The Lost Continent	*Tenant's intent? To hit locals*
The Bedford Incident	*Not if bidet drenched*
Behold A Pale Horse	*Oh hell, bored as ape*
Beyond The Poseidon Adventure	*No! Bonehead devoured petty sin*
Call Of The Wild	*Fellow lad itch*
Paper Tiger	*Ripper gate*
The Cassandra Crossing	*Sardonic gnashers cast*
The Charge Of The Light Brigade	*Here! A large bitch dogfight*
The Day Of The Jackal	*Jack, the deathly oaf*
Deliverance	*Eviler dance*
Royal Flash	*A rash folly*
The Four Musketeers	*Three future smokes*
The Satan Bug	*Ugh! Ant-beast!*
Golden Rendezvous	*Logs doze unnerved*
Grand Theft Auto	*Drat! Not fat, huge!*
The Last American Hero	*Ha ha! A cretin molester*
The Man Who Would Be King	*Ugh! Now I am the lewd knob*
The Mercenaries	*Meaner heretics*
One Spy Too Many	*O my! Spot anyone?*
Escape From Alcatraz	*Malefactor zaps race*
The Poseidon Adventure	*No! The devoured panties!*
Puppet On A Chain	*Phone up captain*

ACTON FILMS OF THE 1980S & 1990S

Silver Dream Racer	*Mere rascal driver*
Die Hard With A Vengeance	*Achieve wandering death*
Runaway Train	*Warn airy aunt*
Romancing The Stone	*Nothing to menacers*
Raise The Titanic	*It is a cretin hate*
Raiders Of The Lost Ark	*Drat! Foolish streaker*
The Punisher	*This pure hen*
The Mosquito Coast	*Comets hoist quota*
Under Fire	*I'd run free*
Die Hard	*Had ride*
The Journey Of The Natty Gann	*Enjoy naughty rotten fat hen*
Indiana Jones And The Last Crusade	*Oh Jesus! Alienated and rancid ants*
Indiana Jones And The Temple Of Doom	*Oh man no! Self-adjoint dope dementia*
The Hunt For Red October	*The defunct hero brother*
High Road To China	*Hoorah! Acid night*
Gleaming The Cube	*Ugh! Blame genetic*
Broken Arrow	*OK, brown rear*
Flesh And Blood	*Ha! Fondled slob*
The Emerald Forest	*Eh? Molester farted*
The Delta Force	*Ho! Elected fart*
Lethal Weapon	*Loath new plea*
Days Of Thunder	*Oh, drafty nudes*
Mission Impossible	*Pessimism is on boil*
Conan The Barbarian	*Na! Bath on nicer arab*
Big Trouble In Little China	*'Unintelligible trio' batch*

AMERICAN FILM ACTORS

Woody Harelson	*Dear loony show*
Harvey Keitel	*Key evil hater*
Sylvester Stallone	*Over talentless Sly*
Tommy Lee Jones	*Let's enjoy memo*
Warren Beaty	*Watery banter*
Kris Kristofferson	*Risk foreskin frost*
Leonardo DiCaprio	*O! Paranoid ice lord*
Michael Keaton	*The coke animal*
Michael Douglas	*He's loud, magical*
Patrick Swayze	*Wears tacky zip*
Richard Gere	*Rich red rage*
Steve Martin	*I'm star event*
Al Pacino	*An oil cap*
Andy Garcia	*A grainy cad*
Antonio Banderas	*No brains on a date*
Arnold Swarzenegger	*He's grown large 'n' crazed*
Bruce Willis	*Slice Wilbur*
Gary Oldman	*Groan madly*
Harrison Ford	*Finds a horror*
Eddie Murphy	*I'm rude, hyped*
Keanu Reeves	*A severe nuke*
Christopher Walken	*Howler stinker chap*
Charlie Sheen	*Na! He is lecher*
Christian Slater	*Latrines this car*
River Phoenix	*Hire pro-vixen*

AMERICAN FILM ACTRESSES

Juliette Lewis	*Lit jewel suite*
Sharon Stone	*Not on her ass*
Sigourney Weaver	*Your views enrage*
Alicia Silverstone	*Erotica Villainess*
Andie MacDowell	*Lewd demoniacal*
Bette Midler	*Diet? Tremble!*
Demi Moore	*Moodier me*
Diane Keaton	*I need oak tan*
Drew Barrymore	*Merry wardrobe*
Uma Thurman	*Unhurt mama*
Jane Seymour	*Same journey*
Julia Roberts	*Just a broiler*
Meg Ryan	*My anger*
Melanie Griffith	*Right fee in a film*
Patricia Arquette	*A tart ape critique*
Jennifer Jason Leigh	*Na! Jeer joining flesh*
Carrie-Anne Moss	*American snores*
Geena Davis	*Evading see*
Mimi Rogers	*I'm grim rose*
Isabella Rossellini	*Also sillier lesbian*
Winona Ryder	*Windy on rear*
Sissy Spacek	*Cissy speaks*
Meryl Streep	*Spry elm tree*
Kathleen Turner	*The leaner trunk*
Laura Dern	*Rural dean*

BLACK & WHITE FILMS

The Birth Of A Nation	*Hot fat hibernation*
The Cabinet Of Dr Caligari	*Behold fanatic geriatric*
The Battleship Potemkin	*In the hottest bleak pimp*
Modern Times	*Dire moments*
Blackmail	*Lack a limb*
Whisky Galore	*Weakish glory*
The Ten Commandments	*Hmm! Conned testament*
Triumph Of The Will	*Hitherto full wimp*
In Which We Serve	*Whichever swine*
We Dive At Dawn	*Want dead view*
Pimpernel Smith	*Nip prim helmets*
Paths Of Glory	*Ghastly proof*
The Adventures Of Robin Hood	*Ho ho! Snob devoured fine tart*
All Quiet On The Western Front	*Now settle infrequent harlot*
The Best Years Of Our Lives	*Boastful severity heroes*
The Bank Dick	*Kinked batch*
Bicycle Thieves	*Ice bitches levy*
The Big Sleep	*She be piglet*
Bringing Up Baby	*Na! Burn piggy bib*
Double Indemnity	*Tidy nubile demon*
Children Of Paradise	*Arch-fiend dopes liar*
The Gold Rush	*Thug holders*
La Grande Illusion	*Old singular alien*
I Know Where I'm Going	*Weighing woke minor*
His Girl Friday	*Shy frigid liar*

BRITISH FILM ACTORS

Ewan McGregor	*Grow acne germ*
Sean Connery	*Annoy screen*
Richard E. Grant	*Grr! Rancid hate*
Albert Finney	*Fry, bent alien*
Stephen Fry	*Thy serf pen*
Alan Bates	*Able Satan*
Johnny Lee Miller	*Her jolly linemen*
Sir John Gielgud	*Irish dog jungle*
Simon Callow	*Ill cow moans*
Bob Hoskins	*Oh, Bob sinks*
Peter Cushing	*Septic hunger*
Corin Redgrave	*Recover in drag*
Dennis Christopher	*Shh! Indiscreet porn*
Pete Postlethwaite	*Swept the ape toilet*
Daniel Day Lewis	*Wide lady aliens*
Michael Caine	*I'm a nice leach*
Bond Star Roger Moore	*Bedroom groaner's rot*
Ian McKellern	*Melanin clerk*
George Arliss	*I large ogress*
Actor Jeremy Irons	*No! I'm a sorry reject*
Leslie Howard	*A weirdo's hell*
Nigel Davenport	*Pentagon drivel*
Ben Cross	*Nob cress*
Nigel Havers	*Girl's heaven*
Ian Charleson	*Crash on alien*

BRITISH FILM ACTRESSES

Margaret Rutherford	*Terror farm daughter*
Actress Minnie Driver	*Cretin's visa reminder*
Anna Friel	*Finer anal*
Glenda Jackson	*Mend jackal's pong*
Kate Winslet	*Ate twinkles*
Catherine Zeta Jones	*The satanic jeer zone*
Kristin Scott Thomas	*Smooth tart isn't sick*
Charlotte Coleman	*Total romance lech*
Anna Chancellor	*Lone clan anarch*
Dame Judi Dench	*Chided nude jam*
Emma Thompson	*Phantom memos*
Eileen Atkins	*Seen alien kit*
Cherie Lunghi	*Higher nuclei*
Rachel Weisz	*Whiz cereals*
Helena Botham Carter	*Abhorrent lame cheat*
Julie Andrews	*Injures a lewd*
Elisabeth Bergner	*Been terrible shag*
Claire Bloom	*I'm local bore*
Madeleine Carroll	*I am recalled loner*
Julie Christie	*Jilts icier hue*
Dame Edith Evans	*Demand heaviest*
Gracie Fields	*Sad lice grief*
Dame Gracie Fields	*Disgrace idle fame*
Rachel Roberts	*Short cerebral*
Margaret Lockwood	*Mega doctoral work*

COMEDY FILMS BEFORE 1960

The Admirable Crichton	*Hitler romanced a bitch*
Abbot And Costello Meet Frankenstein	*Fanatical rottenness entombed bloke*
Animal Crackers	*Lacks manic rear*
And Baby Makes Three	*Hey, smart baked bean*
Ask A Policeman	*An amok special*
Doctor At Large	*A cold ogre tart*
The Belles Of St Trinians	*Talentless shiftier nob*
Blithe Spirit	*Is brittle hip*
Bringing Up Baby	*In grubby pig ban*
Carry On Sergeant	*Arrogant scenery*
The Man In the White Suit	*Huh! I'm in twentieth seat*
A Day At The Races	*Yeah! Cased a tart*
Doctor In The House	*Hot seduction hero*
Duck Soup	*So suck up*
Father Of The Bride	*The horrid beef fat*
The Great Dictator	*Gotcha! Dire tatter*
The Happiest Day Of Your Life	*Hey, this fat ape profiled you!*
Heaven Can Wait	*What naive acne*
The Flying Deuce	*Seduce if lengthy*
The Importance Of Being Earnest	*One fearsome penetrating bitch*
It Happened One Night	*Eh! Diet not happening*
It's A Wonderful World	*Underworld waif's lot*
A Night At The Opera	*Aha! Hate rotten pig*
The Ladykillers	*Sky altered hill*
Road To Singapore	*Good reparations*

COMEDY FILMS OF THE 1960S

What's New Pussycat	*Why cutest saw snap*
A Shot In The Dark	*Ha ha! Rotten kids*
The April Fools	*Pile of harlots*
The Apartment	*Rampant teeth*
Lord Love A Duck	*Old vodka ulcer*
The Nutty Professor	*Hottest person fury*
The Odd Couple	*Hope to cuddle*
The Millionaires	*Ministerial hole*
The Little Shop Of Horrors	*Ho ho! Topless terror filth*
Bob, Ted, Carol And Alice	*O dear! Accidental blob*
How To Murder Your Wife	*Ho! Future wormy weirdo*
Inspector Clouseau	*Secures copulation*
The Great St Trinians Train Robbery	*Entertaining shabby terror artist*
A Guide For The Married Man	*I'm iron-hearted mega fraud*
Barefoot In The Park	*Rotten freak phobia*
Dr Strangelove	*Ardent grovels*
Follow That Camel	*Call hot fowl mate*
The Family Way	*Ya! A filthy mew*
The Disorderly Orderly	*Hey! Older riddler story*
Divorce American Style	*Severely romantic acid*
Carry On Spying	*Scary pony ring*
Carry On Doctor	*Dry croon actor*
Carry On Cleo	*Clay coroner*
Boy, Did I Get A Wrong Number	*O my god! Bed-burning waiter*
The Film Billy Liar	*I'm liberally filth*

COMEDY FILMS OF THE 1970S

The Bad News Bears	*Bashed new breast*
The Bed Sitting Room	*I'm the bigoted snort*
Blazing Saddles	*Dazed ball sings*
California Suite	*Action is failure*
The Front Page	*The after-pong*
Fun With Dick And Jane	*Fine! What candid junk!*
Harold and Maude	*Dread human load*
High Anxiety	*Hi! Hi! Next Gay*
The Kentucky Fried Movie	*Theived fine mock-turkey*
The Life Of Brian	*A fine filth bore*
Love And Death	*The vandal ode*
Love At First Bite	*Beat Soviet flirt*
Meatballs	*Lame blast*
Monty Python And The Holy Grail	*My ninth deathly Anthropology*
National Lampoon's Animal House	*Oh man! Palestinian loon manuals*
The Owl And The Pussycat	*Today, staunchest whelp*
The Pink Panther Strikes Again	*Ha ha! Skip penetrating stinker*
The Return of the Pink Panther	*Inherent funk threat prophet*
Sitting Ducks	*Dusting stick*
Silent Movie	*Moisten evil*
Smoky And The Bandit	*Hated tiny mad knobs*
Every Which Way But Loose	*Ouch! Twelve haywire boys*
They Might Be Giants	*Eight-tenths bigamy*
There's A Girl In My Soup	*Roguishly mean priest*
Travels With My Aunt	*Shy evil mutant wart*

COMEDY FILMS OF THE 1980S

Young Einstien	*One tiny genius*
Working Girl	*Irking growl*
A Fish Called Wanda	*Handles facial wad*
Who Framed Roger Rabbit?	*Bright bedroom warfare*
Trading Places	*Pact earns gild*
The Trail of the Pink Panther	*Knife the philanthrope tart*
Turner and Hooch	*On hard-core hunt*
This Is Spinal Tap	*Hip Satanist lisp*
Throw Momma From The Train	*Earthworm in mammoth fort*
Spies Like Us	*Uses silk pie*
The Secret Of My Success	*Fetch eco-system curses*
Ruthless People	*Hell! Upset poser*
Risky Business	*Is sissy bunker*
Police Academy	*I am a dope cycle*
Planes, Trains and Automobiles	*Onion-dealer's substantial map*
A Private Function	*Vain putrefaction*
Pee-Wee's Big Adventure	*United Beverages weep*
Personal Services	*Clever aspersions*
National Lampoon's European Vacation	*Animal-lover announces a potato piano*
The Naked Gun	*Negated hunk*
The Man With Two Brains	*Banishment worth wait*
Married To The Mob	*I'm the boredom rat*
Lost In America	*Realistic moan*
Look Who's Talking	*OK, allow stink hog*
Gregory's Girl	*Sorry, giggler*
The Gods Must Be Crazy	*Obstructed hazy gems*

CULT FILMS

A Clockwork Orange	*Go conceal ark-work*
The Film Taxi Driver	*Evil X-rated hitfirm*
Teenagers From Outer Space	*Presence of a gruesome tart*
Teenage Cavemen	*Vengeance? Eat me!*
This Is Spinal Tap	*It is ash-pits plan*
Twin Peaks: Fire Walk With Me	*Wealthiest wimp knew fakir*
American Werewolf In London	*Now infernal lower demoniac*
Valley Of The Dolls	*Hell! Lovely fat sod*
Videodrome	*Derive doom*
Way Of The Dragon	*Now fathead orgy*
The Great Rock 'n' Roll Swindle	*Grin well to harlot rednecks*
The Wicker Man	*The main wreck*
Wild In The Streets	*This lewd interest*
Black Frankenstein	*Fickle banner stank*
Cleopatra Jones	*Cajole earns pot*
The Cook, The Thief, His Wife And Her Lover	*Fivefold treacheries — oh, think thee who?*
Armour Of God	*Foam door rug*
Drugstore Cowboy	*Guy borrowed cost*
Enter The Dragon	*Ha! Rotten gender*
Eraserhead	*Sheared ear*
The Last Highway	*Hits wealthy hag*
The Girl Can't Help It	*Hell! Ethnic tart pig*
Killer In High Heels	*Hiring hellish leek*
Rebel Without A Clause	*Auto allure bewitches*
Man Called Horse	*Sad romance hell*

FAMOUS DIRECTORS

Steven Spielberg	*Best spleen giver*
Fatty Arbuckle	*Bulky artefact*
Richard Attenborough	*Hurrah to bored acting!*
Ingmar Bergman	*Ban grim German*
Bernardo Bertolucci	*Nice doctoral rubber*
Jane Campion	*Join acne map*
Francis Ford Coppola	*Flop for sardonic cap*
David Cronenberg	*Covered branding*
George Lucas	*Ace slug ogre*
Blake Edwards	*Weak bladders*
Sir Alfred Hitchcock	*Check focal third*
Stanley Kubrick	*Sick lanky brute*
Mister David Lynch	*My! —Christ and devil*
Alexander Mackendrick	*Marx declined rank cake*
Martin Scorsese	*Screen is a storm*
Sidney Poitier	*Poetry inside*
Roberto Rossellini	*Interior loser slob*
Mel Brooks	*Lob smoker*
Ridley Scott	*Dirty closet*
Sam Peckinpah	*I'm cheap spank*
Alan Parker	*A real prank*
Orson Welles	*Now roleless*
Vincente Minnelli	*I'll invent nice men*
Sidney Lumet	*Timely nudes*
Sir David Lean	*Is dire vandal*

DISNEY FILMS

The Jungle Book	*'Blue thong' joke*
Beauty And The Beast	*Baby at haunted tees*
The Lion King	*Like nothing*
Return To Witch Mountain	*Mutant choir now nuttier*
The Little Mermaid	*Dim lethal termite*
Lady And The Tramp	*Halt mad pedantry*
Winnie The Pooh And Christmas Too	*Ha ha! Tormented this cow opinions*
Aladdin	*In 'lad' ad*
Escape From Witch Mountain	*Whoops! Fierce mutant manic*
The Love Bug	*Huge TV lobe*
White Fang	*Fat whinge*
The Fox And The Hound	*Ho ho! Next death fund*
The Hunchback Of Notre Dame	*Ha ha! End-of-month erect buck*
One Hundred And One Dalmations	*Men unloaded a ironhanded snot*
Mary Poppins	*A snippy romp*
Alice In Wonderland	*Lewd Draconian line*
Snow White And The Seven Dwarfs	*Seventeenth downward sawfish*
Dumbo The Elephant	*Let bonehead thump*
The Aristocats	*Atheist actors*
Hercules	*He's cruel*
Candleshoe	*Leach nodes*
Oliver And Company	*Rod, Navy Policeman*
Simba's Pride	*I impress bad*
The Film Fantasia	*Families that fan*
Steamboat Willie	*Ole! Amiable twits*

FILM MUSICALS

Jolson Sings Again	*Joins on gas signal*
The Major And Minor	*Joint harmed Roman*
The Sound Of Music	*Hideous scum font*
The Wizard Of Oz	*Whiz froze toad*
In The Good Old Summertime	*Delightsome tedium moron*
A Star Is Born	*Brain-rot ass*
The Barkleys Of Broadway	*Weary fat hooky dabblers*
High Society	*His itchy ego*
The Umbrellas of Cherbourg	*Gruesome half-brother club*
The Rocky Horror Picture Show	*Copywriter chokes horror hut*
West Side Story	*I destroy stews*
My Fair Lady	*I am yard fly*
Singin' In The Rain	*Inheriting sin? Na!*
Lady Sings The Blues	*Dashingly tubeless*
That's Entertainment	*Nine-tenths meat tart*
Saturday Night Fever	*Dirty after-shave gun*
Can't Stop The Music	*Champions test cut*
The Harvey Girls	*Ghastly river, eh?*
Invitation To The Dance	*Initiated hot covenant*
Me And My Gal	*Mangled May*
Easter Parade	*Arrested a ape*
Babes In Arms	*Bribe ass man*
Summer Stock	*Rot muck mess*
Swing Time	*Mite's wing*
The Blues Brothers	*Rubber teeth slosh*

ROMANCE FILMS

Breakfast at Tiffanys	*Bats fifty karate films*
Shadowlands	*Now slash dad*
Time After Time	*I'm termite fate*
A Matter Of Life And Death	*A fine fathead tart model*
Heaven Can Wait	*What naive acne!*
Sleepless In Seattle	*Sees talentless pile*
The Bridges Of Madison County	*Oh my god! Fornicated in tubes*
From Here To Eternity	*The rot-free enormity*
A Kind Of Loving	*OK via fondling*
Splendor In The Grass	*Slanderer! This pongs!*
Twice In A Lifetime	*Intimate lice, wife?*
Message In A Bottle	*Amenable egotists*
White Palace	*Aha! Lice wept*
The Great Gatsby	*Begs the gay tart*
Fear Eats The Soul	*The fearless auto*
When Harry Met Sally	*Hell! My trash yawner*
Legends Of The Fall	*Hell! Dangle off set!*
The Gold Rush	*Hog herd slut*
Forces Of Nature	*Cease or turn off!*
The Eye Of The Needle	*Delete the honey fee*
Brief Encounter	*Fine corner tube*
Desert Hearts	*Rested haters*
You've Got Mail	*A vomit eulogy*
Edward Scissorhands	*Darn odd crass wishes*
Ninotchka	*A thin conk*

FILM WESTERNS

Drums Along The Mohawk	*Ho-Hum! Down-market slag*
The Great Train Robbery	*Hotter barbarity genre*
My Darling Clementine	*Incidentally germ men*
The Covered Wagon	*Revenged a hot cow*
Dances With Wolves	*Wow! Enslaves ditch*
Unforgiven	*Fun over gin*
Stagecoach	*Ace hog acts*
The Ox-bow Incident	*No bewitched toxin*
The Gunfighter	*Huge ring theft*
The Searchers	*Three chasers*
The Iron Horse	*Heroine rats*
Butch Cassidy And The Sundance Kid	*Decadent husband's acidity chunks*
The Beguiled	*Eh? Diet bulge*
The Outlaw Josey Wales	*Wow! Let's hate jealousy*
Heaven's Gate	*Aha! Gets even*
The Wild Bunch	*Lunch with bed*
Junior Bonner	*Rejoin unborn*
This Gun For Hire	*Hero ruins Fight*
Broken Arrow	*A born worker*
Northwest Passage	*A wet gnashers spot*
The Far Country	*Ho! Fart century*
Taza, Son Of Cochise	*Fanatics chose zoo*
Gunfight At The OK Corral	*Choking grateful throat*
Pursued	*Rude pus*
High Noon	*Oh! Hog inn*

GANGSTER FILMS

Little Caesar	*Stale article*
The Public Enemy	*Nice humble type*
Smart Money	*My! A Monster*
Lady Killer	*Likely lard*
Kiss Of Death	*Sod this fake*
The Petrified Forest	*Prettier hide offset!*
Bullets Or Ballots	*Tall lout slobbers*
Angels With Dirty Faces	*Weirdest flashy acting*
King of the Underworld	*Renowned OK drug filth*
The Roaring Twenties	*He interrogates twin*
Castle on the Hudson	*Oh no! Student leachs*
Each Dawn I Die	*Acid-head wine*
The Asphalt Jungle	*Hell! The just pagan*
The Enforcer	*Oh! Erect fern*
I Died A Thousand Times	*I'm a sad idiot enthused*
The St. Valentine's Day Massacre	*Heavens! Castrate nasty slime*
This Gun For Hire	*Higher fortune*
Key Largo	*Orgy leak*
The Big Shot	*Bets to high*
The Amazing Dr. Clitterhouse	*Notarize light-hearted scum*
I Walk Alone	*OK alien law*
Kiss Tomorrow Goodbye	*Worrisome stodgy book*
The Desperate Hours	*The sure hated poser*
High Sierra	*Hag is hirer*
Johnny Apollo	*Oh no! Jolly nap!*
You Can Get Away With Murder	*Wow! Hurrah! Decaying mutate*

HORROR FILMS OF THE 1960S & 1970S

Psycho	*Shy cop*
Deranged	*Raged end*
The Texas Chainsaw Massacre	*Sex-maniac teachers — what ass!*
The Exorcist	*Heroic texts*
Monster Of Terror	*Torment of Errors*
The Shuttered Room	*The tortured homes*
The Dunwich Horror	*No! Horrid chew hurt*
The Devil Rides Out	*The tedious drivel*
The Lost Continent	*Clothes intent... not*
To The Devil A Daughter	*Outdated health giver*
Halloween	*O! A new hell*
Ridley Scott's 'Alien'	*Sinisterly located*
Village Of The Damned	*Flog mean hated devil*
The House That Screamed	*Ho-hum! The tart deceases*
Damien, Omen Two	*Now I demon mate*
The Blood Beast Terror	*Bored? Rotate brothels!*
Black Sunday	*Sad yank club*
The Horrible Dr Highcock	*Oh! Check horrid blighter*
The Pit And The Pendulum	*Pundit hunted help-mate*
The Faceless Monster	*False rotten schemes*
Countess Dracula	*Nude lout carcass*
Dracula Prince Of Darkness	*Feared cardinal sucks porn*
Diary Of A Madman	*An odd Mafia army*
The Comedy Of Terrors	*Destroy mother force*
The Haunting	*Hate hunting*

HORROR FILMS OF THE 1980s & 1990s

The Blair Witch Project	*Crew jilt phobic threat*
Silence Of The Lambs	*I'm fat boneless lech*
Event Horizon	*Hero in TV zone*
The Candyman	*Damn thy acne*
Children Of The Corn	*The chronic fondler*
Interview With The Vampire	*I'm with white naive pervert*
Demon Knight	*Get monk hind*
The Silent Scream	*Let's shame cretin*
A Nightmare On Elm Street	*Angel/Saint thermometer*
Night Of The Living Dead	*No! Hated devil fighting*
Friday The Thirteenth	*Thy inherited the fart*
From Dusk Till Dawn	*Damn! Wild fork slut*
Alone In The Dark	*I OK neanderthal*
Creepshow	*Cow herpes*
From A Whisper To A Scream	*Smartarse pro, macho wife*
Dead Ringers	*Regarded sin*
The Dead Zone	*The dazed one*
Body Snatchers	*Deaths by scorn*
Hellraiser	*Real relish*
Lord Of Illusions	*Ill sod ruins fool*
Howl Of The Devil	*He'd flow hot evil*
The Hitcher	*He hit retch*
Dawn Of The Dead	*Odd new fathead*
The Crow	*Chew rot*
Pet Sematary	*Pay teamster*

JAMES BOND FILMS & CHARACTERS

Ernst Stavro Blofeld	*Overall, fronts debts*
James Bond	*Demons jab*
Miss Moneypenny	*Messy ninny poem*
Tatian Romonova	*O man! Rat ovation*
Tiffany Case	*Ya! Stiff acne*
Holly Goodhead	*Oh hell! Gay dodo*
Mary Goodnight	*Oh my! Gonad grit*
Pussy Galore	*Ugly as poser*
Felix Leiter	*Exile trifle*
Rosa Klebb	*Break slob*
Ali Karim Bey	*I like my Arab*
Scaramanga	*Maracas nag*
Casino Royale	*A scary loonie*
Gold Finger	*Fondler gig*
Tomorrow Never Dies	*O, over-weird monster!*
From Russia With Love	*I'm the sorrowful visa*
Thunderball	*Handle blurt*
You Only Live Twice	*Yo! Win lovely cutie*
The Film 'For Your Eyes Only'	*Oh my! Foully eerie Y-fronts*
On Her Majesty's Secret Service	*Severs romantic cheesy jester*
Diamonds Are Forever	*Dreamers invade roof*
Live And Let Die	*Dateline devil*
The Man With The Golden Gun	*Nude mate now thigh-length*
The Spy Who Loved Me	*Elves who doped myth*
Moonraker	*Rank Romeo*

OSCAR WINNING & NOMINEE ACTORS OF THE 1960S

Trevor Howard	*Had terror vow*
Peter Ustinov	*Puniest voter*
Peter O'Toole	*Rot loo tepee*
Marcello Mastroianni	*Romantic animal loser*
Albert Finney	*Banter finely*
Lee Tracy	*Lay erect*
Melvyn Douglas	*Ugly lad's venom*
Richard Burton	*I burnt orchard*
Hugh Griffith	*Hit gruff high*
Anthony Quinn, actor	*Na! horny cannot quit*
Actor Frank Finlay	*Na! yank fart frolic*
Edmund O'Brien	*I burned demon*
Martin Balsam	*Blast Mr mania*
Tom Courtenay	*O my! acne tutor*
Lee Marvin	*Eviler man*
Rod Steiger	*Direst ogre*
Oskar Weiner	*Senior wreak*
Paul Scofield	*Foul lad spice*
Alan Arkin	*A rank nail*
Walter Matthau	*Halt wet trauma*
George Segal	*Ogre gas glee*
Dustin Hoffman	*In off-hand smut*
George Kennedy	*Dyke gone green*
Cliff Robertson	*Nob flirts force*
Mister John Wayne	*His war enjoyment*

OSCAR WINNING ACTORS BEFORE 1960

Lionel Barrymore	*Really minor bore*
Clark Gable	*Black glare*
Charles Laughton	*The carnal ghouls*
Spencer Tracy	*Try crap scene*
James Stewart	*Jeer mass twat*
Gary Cooper	*Yo! Crap ogre*
James Cagney	*Jam gay scene*
Charlton Heston	*Channel's hot rot*
Alec Guiness	*Genuine class*
Marlon Brando	*Darn! Moral nob*
Ernest Borgnine	*Bores inner gent*
Frank Sinatra	*Stink ran afar*
Mister Anthony Quinn	*Harms ninny quotient*
Karl Malden	*Me drank all*
Walter Huston	*Not the walrus*
George Sanders	*Enlarged ogress*
Film star Yul Brynner	*My! Terribly fun snarl*
William Holden	*Hello! I wild man*
Humphrey Bogart	*Hey! Ugh! Brat romp*
Laurence Olivier	*'Air violence' rule*
Ronald Colman	*A droll con man*
Bing Crosby	*In BBC's orgy*
Broderick Crawford	*Reward for bird cock*
Burl Ives	*Evil rubs*
Hugh Griffith	*Hit high gruff*

OSCAR WINNING & NOMINEE ACTORS OF THE 1970S

James Whitmore	*The Jaws memoir*
Melvyn Douglas	*Ugly lad's venom*
Actor John Mills	*Major snot chill*
Gary Busey	*Gay buyers*
Gene Hackman	*Heck! Mean nag*
Peter Finch	*I French pet*
Eddie Albert	*Deliberated*
Robert Duvall	*Bald lover rut*
Al Pacino	*An oil cap*
Actor Jack Lemmon	*Major comet clank*
Randy Quaid	*A randy quid*
Art Carney	*Trance ray*
Robert De Niro	*Error on bidet*
Lee Strasberg	*Largest beers*
George Burns	*Snore bugger*
Jack Nicholson	*Join shock clan*
Maximillian Schell	*Hillman mixes lilac*
Jason Robards	*Ran a dross job*
Burt Young	*Guy nob rut*
Richard Dreyfuss	*Dreads fish curry*
Peter Firth	*Riper theft*
Jon Voight	*Join TV hog*
Jack Warden	*Cranked jaw*
Frederic Forrest	*Stiffer recorder*
Justin Henry	*Is Jenny hurt?*

OSCAR WINNING & NOMINEE ACTORS OF THE 1980S

Timothy Hutton	*Him nutty tooth*
Robert Preston	*Born protester*
Michael O'Keefe	*Oi! Female cheek*
Henry Fonda	*A horny fend*
Dudley Moore	*Yo! Rude model*
Tom Conti	*I'm cotton*
Ben Kingsley	*Kneel by sign*
Louis Gosset JR	*Glorious jests*
John Lithgow, actor	*No harlot witch jog*
Tom Courtenay	*O man! Cutey rot*
Albert Finney	*Fry bent alien*
British actor John Hurt	*Just a thin horror bitch*
F. Murray Abraham	*Ha! Marry a far bum*
Jeff Bridges, actor	*Forged fabric jest*
Tom Hulce	*Home cult*
Sam Waterston	*Now a tart mess*
William Hurt	*Um, ill wraith?*
Harrison Ford	*Finds a horror*
Dexter Gordon	*Next dog order*
Dennis Hopper	*Enshrined pop*
Michael Douglas	*Sad malice ghoul*
Denzel Washington	*Na! Lewd night's zone*
James Ivory	*I've rosy jam*
River Phoenix	*Rip vixen hero*
Martin Landau	*Mad urinal tan*

OSCAR ACTORS 1990S

Gerard Depardieu	*Degraded pure air*
Kevin Costner	*Sickener on TV*
Bruce Davison	*Absurd novice*
Andy Garcia	*A grainy cad*
Actor Richard Harris	*Horrid rat's car chair*
Tom Cruise	*So I'm cuter*
Tommy Lee Jones	*Me enjoy motels*
Harvey Keitel	*Key evil-hater*
Michael Lerner	*Chiller near me*
Jack Palance	*Jap lack acne*
Anthony Hopkins	*No! Posh thin yank*
Nick Nolte	*I lent conk*
Robert Downey Jr	*Retry wonder job*
Stephen Rea	*Neat herpes*
Jaye Davidson	*Adds naive joy*
David Paymer	*A very mad dip*
Tom Hanks	*Monk's hat*
Mel Gibson	*Big melons*
Nicholas Cage	*I conceal shag*
Tim Robbins	*I bit Mr snob*
Morgan Freeman	*Former mean nag*
Mister Sean Penn	*Meanest spinner*
Matt Damon	*Madman tot*
Actor Ben Affleck	*Black acne effort*
Ralph Fiennes	*Replenish fan*

OSCAR WINNING & NOMINEE ACTRESSES OF THE 1960S

Natalie Wood	*I wanted a loo*
Shirley Jones	*Jeer holy sins*
Shirley Maclaine	*Nicely male hairs*
Geraldine Page	*Need a large pig*
Rita Moreno	*Irate moron*
Anne Bancroft	*Ban front acne*
Katharine Ross	*Stark as heroin*
Thelma Ritter	*Hitler matter*
Melinda Mercouri	*Delirium romance*
Debbie Reynolds	*Blind, seedy bore*
Agnes Moorehead	*Oh dear! Mega-nose!*
Kim Stanley	*I smelt yank*
Lila Kedrova	*A overall kid*
Gladys Cooper	*A godly corpse*
Samantha Eggar	*The gas anagram*
Elizabeth Hartman	*Harm in battle haze*
Shelley Winters	*Tiny sewer hells*
Lynne Redgrave	*Randy leg nerve*
Ida Kaminski	*Sink a kid aim*
Ruth Gordon	*Dour throng*
Vivien Merchant	*Inventive charm*
Jean Simmons	*Join mass men*
Estelle Parsons	*Stolen leper ass*
Joanne Woodward	*Adorn wooden jaw*
Maggie Smith	*I'm mega sight*

OSCAR WINNING ACTRESSES BEFORE 1960

Ethel Barrymore	*Merely abort her*
Ingrid Bergman	*Grim danger bin*
Mary Pickford	*Firm porky cad*
Katharine Hepburn	*The piranha bunker*
Claudette Colbert	*Collect brute date*
Bette Davis	*A vet's bidet*
Hattie McDaniel	*I'm a hated client*
Shelley Winters	*Tiny sewers hell*
Vivien Leigh	*Evil gin hive*
Joanne Woodward	*Adorn wooden jaw*
Grace Kelly	*Clergy leak*
Luise Rainer	*Airline user*
Ms Joan Crawford	*Major fan crowds*
Olivia de Havilland	*Aha! Odd evil villain*
Ms Judy Holliday	*Ha! Is jolly muddy*
Susan Hayward	*Dash runaways*
Jane Wyman	*Jaw any men*
Greer Garson	*Grrr! Sane ego*
Gloria Grahame	*I am a larger hog*
Eva Marie Saint	*I'm a native arse*
Kim Hunter	*Tinker hum*
Donna Reed	*Darned one*
Loretta Young	*A gutter loony*
Miss Ginger Rogers	*Ogress grime rings*
Audrey Hepburn	*Nude harp buyer*

OSCAR WINNING & NOMINEE ACTRESSES OF THE 1970S

Tatum O'Neal	*Ole! A mutant*
Louise Fletcher	*I felt lecherous*
Jane Alexander	*Axed annal jeer*
Helen Hayes	*Hyena heels*
Maureen Stapleton	*Sole apeman nutter*
Diane Ladd	*An idle dad*
Jane Fonda, actress	*Adjacent sore fans*
Cicely Tyson	*On itsy cycle*
Gena Rowlands	*Na! Lewd organs*
Marsha Mason	*Sham as roman*
Sylvia Sidney	*Envy dialysis*
Linda Blair	*I bland liar*
Ellen Burnstyn	*Nun's entry bell*
Valerie Perrine	*Near virile peer*
Valentina Cortese	*Sane tart violence*
Ronee Blakley	*Lonely beaker*
Sissy Spacek	*Seasick spys*
Beatrice Straight	*A big heretic's tart*
Piper Laurie	*Puerile pair*
Talia Shire	*I hate liars*
Vanessa Redgrave	*Never ravaged ass*
Melinda Dillon	*Inane mild doll*
Penelope Milford	*I'm people fondler*
Barbara Barrie	*Briar area barb*
Sally Field	*False idyll*

OSCAR WINNING & NOMINEE ACTRESSES OF THE 1980S

Mary Steenburgen	*Megabyte runners*
Cathy Moriarty	*Oh! I'm a tarty cry*
Diana Scarwid	*In sad acid war*
Joan Hackett	*Can that joke*
Jessica Lange	*Ace ass jingle*
Amy Madigan	*Damn! I am gay*
Lesley Ann Warren	*Na! New sly learner*
Debra Winger	*Brew dire nag*
Linda Hunt	*Nun hit lad*
Alfre Woodard	*A foreword lad*
Actress Judy Davis	*Curvy sadist's jade*
Peggy Ashcroft	*Gasp! Fetch orgy*
Lindsay Crouse	*Snored saucily*
Geraldine Page	*Lingered agape*
Angelica Huston	*The unsocial nag*
Margaret Avery	*At a merry grave*
Dianne Wiest	*Detain swine*
Mary Elizabeth Mastrantonio	*Amazement in this laboratory*
Marlee Matlin	*Male terminal*
Eileen Brennan	*Been near Lenin*
Sigourney Weaver	*Young arse review*
Anne Archer	*Her acne ran*
Tess Harper	*Press hater*
Kim Stanley	*Steamy link*

OSCAR ACTRESSES OF THE 1990S

Marisa Tomei	*I emit aromas*
Catherine Deneuve	*Erect? I heaven, nude*
Kathy Bates	*Tyke ash tab*
Annette Bening	*Bent ant engine*
Lorraine Bracco	*Boo! Carnal crier*
Kim Basinger	*Semi barking*
Susan Sarandon	*Adorn a nun's ass*
Gwyneth Paltrow	*Wow! Lengthy trap*
Mary McDonnell	*Mr Manly cloned*
Holly Hunter	*Thy null hero*
Mercedes Ruehl	*Resumed lecher*
Jessica Tandy	*Inject ass day*
Kate Nelligan	*Angel-like ant*
Actress Judy Davis	*Jesus! Vast dry acid*
Joan Plowright	*Worth jail pong*
Miranda Richardson	*Darn horrid maniacs*
Actress Anna Paquin	*Can pass quarantine*
Debra Winger	*Dire nag brew*
Brenda Fricker	*Crank free bird*
Jodie Foster	*Diets for Joe*
Geena Davis	*Sad vein age*
Frances MacDormand	*Scorn damn mad farce*
Juliette Binoche	*I inject hole tube*
Mira Sorvino	*Minor savior*
Miss Helen Hunt	*Hunts hemlines*

OSCAR WINNING DIRECTORS

Sir Richard Attenborough	*Ugh! It's hard-core brain rot*
Warren Beatty	*Beware tyrant*
Woody Allen	*A lewd loony*
Milos Forman	*A moron's film*
Mister Robert Zemeckis	*Merriest Bizet mockers*
Steven Spielberg	*Leper's big events*
Jonathan Demme	*The Madonna jam*
Oliver Stone	*Violent sore*
Barry Levinson	*Envy born liars*
Bernardo Bertolucci	*Corrected urban boil*
Sydney Pollack	*Slyly naked cop*
Robert Redford	*Bedford terror*
Francis Coppola	*Crap! Fool's panic*
William Friedkin	*Na! If I'm weird...kill!*
David Lean	*Invade lad*
Billy Wilder	*Lewd lily rib*
Frank Capra	*Fan carpark*
Mister John Huston	*Just month's heroin*
Clint Eastwood	*Old west action!*
Kevin Costner	*Sickener on TV*
James L. Brooks	*Job masks role*
Michael Cimino	*Minimal choice*
Mike Nicols	*I'm neck soil*
John Schlesinger	*Shh! Censor jingle!*
Carol Reed	*Old career*

OSCAR WINNING FILMS OF THE 1960S

Midnight Cowboy	*God, now I'm bitchy!*
The Apartment	*Tart nap theme*
West Side Story	*SOS! Dirty sweet*
Lawrence Of Arabia	*A forbearance wail*
My Fair Lady	*I may fry lad*
A Patch Of Blue	*Foul cheap tab*
The Sound Of Music	*Hideous scum font*
A Man For All Seasons	*Nasal roof salesman*
In The Heat Of The Night	*Hate the fine hot thing!*
Oliver	*I lover*
Elmer Gantry	*Manly regret*
Judgment At Nuremberg	*Mutant jug bender germ*
Lilies Of The Field	*Hell! I diet of flies*
True Grit	*Trite rug*
Cat Ballou	*A local, but...*
The Graduate	*Eat daughter*
The Virgin Spring	*Hi! Grr! Invents pig*
Through A Glass Darkly	*Ha! OK sluggardly trash*
Sundays And Sybele	*Ya! Bad sly nudeness*
Yesterday, Today And Tomorrow	*Now do a moody, starry-eyed tart*
The Shop On Main Street	*This mean potent horse*
The Miracle Worker	*Leatherwork crime*
Closely Observed	*Cosy lover bleeds*
War And Peace	*Acne ape ward*
Cactus Flowers	*Foul cast crews*

OSCAR WINNING FILMS OF THE 1970s

The Godfather	*The hog farted*
The Sting	*This gent*
One Flew Over The Cuckoo's Nest	*Choke twelve foot nurse once*
Woody Allen's Annie Hall	*An alien loo's well handy*
The Deer Hunter	*Under her teeth*
The film Kramer Vs Kramer	*Hmmm! Fear rival trekkers*
Save The Tiger	*This eager vet*
Harry And Tonto	*Oh no! Randy tart*
The Goodbye Girl	*Glory be! Diet hog*
Women In Love	*Men view loon*
A Touch Of Class	*Of a slouch cast*
Cabaret	*Ace brat*
Alice Doesn't Live Here Anymore	*Oh no! Really steamier evidence*
Ryan's Daughter	*Huge randy star*
The Last Picture Show	*Let us whip the actors*
The Paper Chase	*Apt; he preaches.*
The Sunshine Boys	*Oh! Teeny bush sins*
All The President's Men	*This resplendent male*
Murder On The Orient Express	*Not pure extreme horridness*
California Suite	*Is action failure*
Butterflies Are Free	*Feeble sure-fire tart*
Paper Moon	*A porn poem*
Being There	*Big hen tree*
Patton: Lust For Glory	*Forgot snotty plural*
The French Connection	*Fetch nice nonce north*

OSCAR WINNING FILMS OF THE 1980S

Ordinary People	*I prepared loony*
Chariots of Fire	*Is of heroic fart*
Terms Of Endearment	*Rotten men defamers*
Out Of Africa	*Ciao! Fat four*
The Last Emperor	*Mere harlot pest*
Driving Miss Daisy	*Dismiss rigid navy*
On Golden Pond	*London ponged*
Tender Mercies	*Redeems cretin*
Kiss Of The Spider Woman	*Safe demon-worship kits*
The Color Of Money	*Oh no! My erect fool!*
Wall Street	*We sell tart*
Coal Miner's Daughter	*Murder-case loathing*
Sophie's Choice	*Ho ho! Sic pieces*
Places In The Heart	*He's parenthetical*
Children Of A Lesser God	*Sold hard-core feelings*
The Trip To Bountiful	*Bite truthful option*
Melvin And Howard	*Landowner had vim*
The Year Of Living Dangerously	*Originally evade huge Y-fronts*
A Passage To India	*Against soap idea*
The Accidental Tourist	*Ethical tart seduction*
Born On The Fourth Of July	*One of truthful horny job*
Cinema Paradiso	*I am sardonic ape*
Moonstruck	*Stuck moron*
A Fish Called Wanda	*Na! A lewd acid flash*
An Officer And A Gentleman	*Face a fan lamenting drone*
The Killing Fields	*Fiends like digit flesh*

OSCAR WINNING FILMS BEFORE 1960

The Quiet Man	*Quaint theme*
Treasure Of The Sierra Madre	*Eerie hat for rude smartarse*
The Westerner	*Rent the sewer*
Bridge On The River Kwai	*Inhibited grave-worker*
On The Waterfront	*Warn of the rotten*
From Here To Eternity	*Theory of retirement*
An American In Paris	*Near aspirin maniac*
Mutiny On The Bounty	*Hey! Nutty bum notion*
Black Orpheus	*Chalks up bore*
The Grapes Of Wrath	*Fat warthog sphere*
Gone With The Wind	*Tonight when wide*
It Happened One Night	*Hate in-depth opening*
A Streetcar Named Desire	*Recreated mean disaster*
The Diary Of Anne Frank	*Oh dear! Fat ninny freak*
Three Faces Of Eve	*Hate coffee verse*
Separate Tables	*Stale apre breast*
The Philadelphia Story	*Shhh! Daily toilet-paper*
Goodbye, Mr Chips	*Hid my bog corpse*
Yankee Doodle Dandy	*Annoyed loaded dyke*
TheAfrican Queen	*Fanatic hen queer*
Cyrano de Bergerac	*Bye! Record carnage*
The Greatest Show On Earth	*Harsh Hottentot sewerage*
Gentleman's Agreement	*Let's mate gangrene men*
Going My Way	*My wig agony*
A Place In The Sun	*Cheap inane slut*
Broadway Melody	*Made bloody wary*

SCI-FI FILMS OF THE 1960S & 1970S

Close Encounters Of The Third Kind	*Host children ride ten cent UFOs, OK?*
Daleks Invasion Earth	*Asks "Annihilate Dover?"*
Crimes Of The Future	*Furies of the rectum*
Sinbad And The Eye Of The Tiger	*Shift dirty teenage bone-head*
The Andromeda Strain	*Drat! Sheer damnation*
Warlords Of Atlantis	*Fatal world arsonist*
The Planet Of The Apes	*Ha! Fat telephone pest*
The Black Hole	*Bleak hot lech*
Capricorn One	*Nice car porno*
Children Of The Damned	*Left-handed rich demon*
Star Wars: A New Hope	*Wear trash weapons*
Damnation Alley	*Not a madly alien*
The Damned	*Death mend*
The Day Of The Triffids	*If hated, destroy fifth*
Escape To Witch Mountain	*O man! pathetic new coitus*
Invasion Of The Body Snatchers	*Oh no! Fascist rent-boy vanished*
Jason And The Argonauts	*Oh Jesus no! Tart and a nag!*
Kingdom Of The Spiders	*Skip frightened dooms*
The Man Who Fell To Earth	*Thrown the loath female*
Mysterious Island	*Adultery missions*
The Omega Man	*Mean hog mate*
Panic In Year Zero	*Prize rainy canoe*
Quatermass And The Pit	*Drat this apeman quest*
Time Machine	*I'm hit menace*
Voyage To The Bottom Of The Sea	*Ho ho! Move to eat fattest bogey*

SCI-FI FILMS OF THE 1980S AND 1990S

Time Bandits	*Damn! It bites!*
The Philadelphia Experiment	*It explained Hitler hemp heap*
Short Circuit	*I court Christ*
Innerspace	*Screen pain*
The Terminator	*I'm rotten hater*
Back To The Future	*Cutthroat UK beef*
Blade Runner - The Directors Cut	*Lucid death scene terror burnt*
Clash Of The Titans	*Aha! Filth contests*
The Dark Crystal	*Shady clerk tart*
Dragon Slayer	*Lady groaners*
E.T. The Extra-Terrestrial	*Alert! The ex-tart retires*
Flash Gordon	*Lands for hog*
Flatliners	*A lens flirt*
The Matrix	*Him ex-tart*
Fight The Future	*Huge fruit theft*
Mad Max Beyond Thunderdome	*Oh no! Damn! Bad muddy extreme*
The Neverending Story	*Sod the tinny revenger*
The Navigator	*A rave tonight*
The Princess Bride	*Cretin breeds ship*
Dreamscape	*Damp crease*
The Empire Strikes Back	*Break thickest premise*
The film Spacecamp	*Catch female pimps*
Highlander	*He hid gnarl*
Total Recall	*Ole! Call tart*
Weird Science	*I screwed nice*

STAR WARS CHARACTERS & ACTORS

The Millenium Falcon	*Me? Hell, I malfunction!*
Natalie Portman	*I am porn talent*
Anakin Skywalker	*Alas, kinky wanker*
Artoo-Detoo	*O! Adore toot!*
Captain Han Solo	*Oh no! Satanic pal*
Alec Guinness	*Genuine Class*
Luke Skywalker	*Weekly sulk ark*
Princess Leia	*Increase lisp*
Darth Vader	*Hard Advert*
Obi-Wan Kenobi	*Noon kiwi babe*
Chewbacca the Wookie	*Oh wow! Big cake cache*
Master Yoda	*Smeary toad*
See Three Pee Oh	*See the hero pee*
Actor Mark Hamill	*Talk, Mr macho liar*
Carrie Fisher	*If richer arse*
Harrison Ford	*Finds a horror*
James Earl Jones	*Jane loses me jar*
Queen Amidala	*A equal maiden*
Darth Sidious	*Ha! Sordid suit*
Darth Maul	*Adult harm*
Senator Palpatine	*Planet separation*
Jedi Master Qui Gonn Jinn	*Men in Inn's Quart jog*
Jake Lloyd	*Dally joke*
Samuel L Jackson	*Same junk locals*
Liam Neeson	*Senile moan*
Ewan Macgregor	*Am careworn egg*

THRILLER FILMS OF THE 1950S, 1960S & 1970S

Murder On The Orient Express	*Muttered expenses in horror*
Play Misty For Me	*My measly profit*
Escape From Alcatraz	*Crap froze a lame cast*
Billion Dollar Brain	*I'll rain on billboard*
Bonnie And Clyde	*No! Cyanide blend*
The Conversation	*Non-creative shot*
Death On The Nile	*Lenient hothead*
Death Wish	*Hashed wit*
Fear Is The Key	*Hey! Freak site*
Funeral In Berlin	*Refine null brain*
The Gauntlet	*He latent gut*
The Getaway	*Wet gay heat*
The Ipcress File	*It is flesh creep*
The Long Good Friday	*Loony dogfight dare*
The Long Goodbye	*Hot golden bogey*
Marathon Man	*Oh man! Rat man*
Point Blank	*Tap on blink*
Rear Window	*Warn weirdo*
The Spy Who Came In From The Cold	*Oh my! Chew elephant discomfort*
Dial M For Murder	*I'm rude farm lord*
Kiss Me Deadly	*Sad dyke slime*
The Man Who Knew Too Much	*Oh wow! Thank the commune*
North By Northwest	*Threw thy born snot*
Slaughter On Tenth Avenue	*Huge heaven-sent lout rant*
Cleopatra Jones	*Reject soap loan*

THRILLER FILMS OF THE 1980S AND 1990S

Basic Instinct	*Sin-bin tactics*
The Big Easy	*He bites gay*
Blown Away	*Now a bylaw*
The Body Guard	*Ha! Dodgy brute*
Clear And Present Danger	*Prenatal gender dancers*
Dressed To Kill	*Oddest killers*
Executive Decision	*Nice sex-video cutie*
Fatal Attraction	*Total fanatic rat*
Final Analysis	*Alias in sly fan*
The Fugitive	*I've thief gut*
Last Man Standing	*Damn! Satan glints*
Magnum Force	*Fun coma germ*
The Fourth Protocol	*Corrupt the hot fool*
The Mirror Cracked	*Rich market record*
Point Of No Return	*Nutrient of porno*
Pulp Fiction	*Clip upon fit*
Reservoir Dogs	*Gross over-ride*
Sea Of Love	*Solve a foe*
Single White Female	*The fine sewage mill*
Entrapment	*Ten rapt men*
Color Of Night	*Frothing loco*
Still Of Night	*It's long filth*
The House On Carroll Street	*Hello to honest heroes*
Evil Under The Sun	*Vile nude hunters*
The Hand That Rocks The Cradle	*Drat! Check athlete shorthand*

BRANDS OF BEER & LAGER

Fuller's London Pride	*Rude fondlers in poll*
Bass Draught Ale	*Head sugar blast*
John Smith's Bitter	*Men thirst this job*
Foster's Ice	*Fierce toss*
William Stone's Bitter	*Obtain smellier twits*
Webster's Yorkshire Bitter	*This bores witty berserker*
McEwan's Export	*Excerpts woman*
Theakston Bitter	*Beat hotter stink*
Flower's Bitter	*Wet flirts bore*
Marston Bitter	*Brimstone tart*
Kilkenny Irish Beer	*Shiny kinkier rebel*
Caffrey's Genuine Draught	*Ensuring a far-fetch guy*
Guinness Draught	*Drug naughtiness*
Guinness Original	*Ensuring a soiling*
Worthington Creamflow	*Now hot gremlin cow fart*
Irish Harp Lager	*Harsher pig liar*
Bank's Draught	*Shag drunk bat*
Newcastle Brown Ale	*Wasn't bowel cleaner*
Stella Artois Lager	*Earlier glass total*
Ruddles English Ale	*He'll dread ugliness*
Younger's Bitter	*Obesity grunter*
Holsten Pills	*Hell! Snot lips*
Heineken Lager	*Ah! Keen leering*
Budweiser Lager	*Bad uglier sewer*
Carlsberg Export	*Grrr! Expect a slob*

BRITISH CUISINE

Battered Fish And Chips	*This drab cheapest find*
Pickled Eggs	*Deck pig's legs*
Yorkshire Pudding	*Horny pudgier kids*
Black Pudding	*Dug bland pick*
Oxford Sausages	*Sugar as sex food*
Spotted Dick	*Odd tick pest*
Isle Of Man Herring Pie	*I'm pleasing finer hero*
Sussex Stewed Steak	*Sexes status skewed*
Boned Roast Sirloin	*Indoors in bloaters*
Cornish Charter Pie	*Protein-rich search*
Cheshire Pork And Apple Pie	*Ha ha! Popped peril sickener*
Devonshire Squab Pie	*Queer invades bishop*
Steak And Kidney Pie	*A destined kinky ape*
Roast Pheasant	*Shapes on a tart*
Boiled Silverside	*Is lovebird diesel*
Lincolnshire Chine	*Nice in hellish corn*
Bradenham Ham	*Ha! Madman herb*
The Ulster Fry	*Utterly fresh*
Toad In The Hole	*Oh no! The detail!*
Cumberland Sausage	*Na! Large abused scum*
Mashed Potato With Dulse	*This somewhot loud adept*
Potted Mushrooms	*Sod summer hotpot!*
Macaroni With Cheese	*I am the choice answer*
Stewed Venison	*No! Invests weed*
Ragout Of Rabbit	*Boo! Tart bug fair*

DESSERTS

Semolina	*Is no meal*
Vanilla Custard Tart	*Drat! Rival Satan cult*
Walnut And Fig Tart	*Fatal rat dung twin*
Strawberries And Cream	*Nicer want embarassed*
Chocolate Fudge Cake	*Catalogued coke chef*
Bramble And Apple Crumble	*Became plump bland barrel*
Bread And Butter Pudding	*Drat! Updated bed-burning*
Caramel Rice Pudding	*Acidic gardener lump*
Hot Mango Souffles	*Gosh! fateful moons*
Passion Fruit Souffles	*Piss off! Nauseous flirt*
White And Dark Chocolate Mouse	*How mad hatter cooked lunacie*
Melon With Summer Fruits	*Twelfth emission murmur*
Fruit Salad	*A fluid star*
Spiced Winter Fruit Compote	*Now imperfect pot crudities*
Rhubarb Crumble	*Rubber club harm*
Cinnamon And Honey Wafers	*Arson now enhanced infamy*
Fruit Terrine	*Urine fritter*
Blueberry Pie	*Bury peer bile*
Summer Pudding	*Drumming dupes*
Raspberry Sorbet	*Barber sorts prey*
Caramel Bananas	*An Arab's manacle*
Iced Hazlenut Mousse	*Demonize a cute slush*
Saffron Meringues	*Suffering moaners*
Lemon Meringue	*Minor menu glee*
Raspberry Mousse Gateau	*Pursue a smartarse bogey*

FRENCH CUISINE

Pear And Hazlenut Flan	*Half-nude Tarzan panel*
Croissants	*I crass snot*
Camembert Fritters	*Remember fit tracts*
Red Onion Galettes	*Oldest generation*
Salade Mouclade	*Dead casual mole*
French Beans	*Chef's banner*
Golden Cheese Puffs	*Scoffed huge spleen*
Salade Nicoise	*Ciao, sad senile*
Garlic Mussels	*Salesgirl scum*
Sole Goujons	*Jesus on logo*
Red Mullet With Fennel	*Run lewd filth element*
Quiche Lorraine	*I core harlequin*
Grilled Sardines	*Darned girl's lies*
French Bread	*Her franc bed*
Trout With Mushroom Sauce	*Ahem! This rum tortuous cow*
Normandy Pheasant	*Hey! Damn Satan porn*
Breton Pork	*Knob report*
Pot Roast Poussins	*It's rat soup-spoons*
Ratatouille	*A retail lout*
Onion Tart	*In no tarot*
Potato Gratin	*Tango patriot*
Chocolate Roulade	*Actual cooled hero*
Crepes Suzette	*Erect Zeus pest*
Tarte Tatin	*Taint treat*
Chocolate Profiteroles	*Orchestrate police fool*

ITALIAN CUISINE

Tuscan Bean Soup	*Pan abuse counts*
Fritto Misto	*Tit fits room*
Marinated Pepper	*Parsnip permeated*
Grilled Proscuitto	*Culprits ogled riot*
Tomato And Mozarella Salad	*No! Amazed total amoral lads*
Spaghetti Bolonese	*Hospitable gent goes*
Spinach Raviolli	*O, sharp civilian*
Pollo Sorprese	*Opposes roller*
Potato Gnocchi	*No! Catch pig too*
Artichoke Pizza	*I hate rock pizza*
Vitello con Funghi	*Foul vein clothing*
Stuffed Sardines	*Disaster snuffed*
Char Grilled Squid	*Grr! Clashed liquid*
Saffron Seafood Risotto	*No! Disaster of roof fatso*
Pigeon On Polenta	*To open alien pong*
Risotto Milanese	*Sinister loo mate*
Beef Braised In Barolo	*Rare baboon disbelief*
Italian Sausages	*It is a slag nausea*
Soft Polenta	*Poof talents*
Asparagus Frittata	*A! Sip a fat sugar tart*
Baked Fennel	*Lank been fed*
Aubergine Gratin	*Bartering guinea*
Garlic Potatoes	*Total coarse pig*
Panna Cotta With Sauce	*Now acute satanic path*
Panforte De Siena	*No! Feared panties*

ORIENTAL AND INDIAN CUISINE

Chinese Spareribs	*Ships arsenic beer*
Chicken Tikka Masala	*Animals hack cake kit*
Chicken Chow Mein	*Nice hen cock whim*
Sweet And Sour Pork	*Keeps wondrous rat*
Fried Sea Slug	*Grease fluids*
Chicken Congee	*Nice geek conch*
Chinese Steamed Fish	*Hen satisfied scheme*
Cantonese Lobster	*Not bloater's scene*
Gingered Vegetables	*Evil beast egg gender*
Tamatar Bharta	*Bahama rat tart*
Chicken Pulao	*Piano chuckle*
Prawn Biryani	*Raw briny pain*
Onion Bhaji	*Oh! Join a bin!*
Vegetable Samosas	*Beast savages mole*
Dry Beef Curry	*Rude cyber fry*
Pork Vindaloo	*Vodka porn oil*
Chicken Korma	*Make conk rich*
Yoghurt Chicken	*Tricky hen cough*
Madras Chicken Curry	*Rancid as cherry muck*
Tandoori Murg	*I'm a dung root*
Shrimp Puloa	*A lumpish pro*
Bangra Masala	*Banal ram saga*
Banana Raita	*Aaa! Ant brain*
Mango Chutney	*Ugh! Not my acne*
Nariel Samosas	*So, animal's arse!*

TYPES & BRANDS OF SPIRITS

Bushmills	*Lush limbs*
Jack Daniels	*Snide jackal*
Captain Morgan Rum	*No! A maturing cramp*
Cream Of The Barley	*Blame hearty force*
Imperial Vodka	*Laid Vampire OK*
Malibu White Rum	*Wear bum lithium*
Whyte And Mackay	*Wacky anthem day*
Gordon's London Gin	*No! Odd long snoring*
Ron Bacardi Superior	*Obscure air-raid porn*
White Satin Gin	*The waiting sin*
Martell Fine Cognac	*Large mean conflict*
Bombay Sapphire Gin	*Shabbier pimp agony*
Remy Martin Champagne	*Impermanent gay charm*
Stone's Cream Liquer	*Quarrelsome incest*
Bailey's Irish Cream	*I'm basic heresy liar*
Cognac Courvoisier	*Voracious coercing*
Tanqueray English Gin	*Earning thy squealing*
Tudor Dry Gin	*Dirty ground*
Plymouth Gin	*Imply nought*
Napoleon Brandy	*Any noble pardon*
William Grant's Whiskey	*I'm stylish raw weakling*
Pernod Fils	*Slop finder*
Black Label Whiskey	*Walks like baby lech*
Glenmorangie Whiskey	*King laying somewhere*
Teacher's Highland Cream	*Gremlins headache chart*

VEGETARIAN CUISINE

Curried Parsnip Soup	*Crisp upper dinosaur*
Vegetable Gumbo	*Movable egg tube*
Lentil Soup	*Pollutes in*
Grapefruit Salad	*Strap a lifeguard*
Marinated Courgettes	*Meager tart seduction*
Guacamole Stuffed Tomatoes	*Foulest fat damage comes out*
Fried Beancurd	*Fine bread crud*
Garlic Mushrooms	*Grim loo-scum rash*
Love Apples	*Leaves plop*
Fusilli With Fresh Tomato Sauce	*This steamier faithful cow soul*
Marrow With Macaroni	*Wow! Romantic arm hair*
Tagliatelle	*Little algae*
Sicilian Pasta	*Is a satanic lip*
Savoury Baked Rice	*Our backyard sieve*
Curried Rice And Peas	*Rude as rancid recipe*
Red Bean Risotto	*Restoration bed*
Mushroom Risotto	*Riotous Mr Smooth*
North African Couscous	*Unconscious roach fart*
Baked Barley	*A key dabbler*
Gujerati Cabbage	*Garbage juice tab*
Tofu With Cashew Nuts	*Watch funhouse twist*
Spinach	*Chap sin*
Mixed Beans	*Debase minx*
Fried Noodles	*Defines drool*
Baked Sweet Potatoes	*Wastebasket too deep*

TYPES OF AIRCRAFT & HELICOPTER

Supermarine Spitfire	*Feminist repairer's up*
Consolidated Liberator	*I blasted erotica drool*
The Grumman Wildcat	*What glum mad cretin*
Republic Thunderjet	*Bitch returned julep*
Boeing Superfortresses	*Bruiser's present goof*
Canberra Bomber	*Embrace born bar*
Boeing Stratofortress	*Target of sorriest snob*
Saab Draken	*Na! Sad break*
Fighting Falcon	*Flinch in faggot*
Super Mirage	*Sugar empire*
McDonnell Douglas Eagle	*Dangled on slag molecule*
Gruman Hawkeye	*Waken huge army*
Sepecht Jaguar	*A huge jet scrap*
Eurofighter	*Huge rot fire*
Shorts Skyvan	*Vast sky horns*
Beechcraft Super King Air	*Pricking the farce abuser*
Canadair Challenger	*Hell! A rancid carnage*
Cessna Skymaster	*Crass Enemy tasks*
Concorde Aircraft	*Infra-red coco cart*
Lockheed Blackbird	*Dickhead blob clerk*
Microjet	*Crime jot*
North American Texan	*Oh man! An extra cretin*
Panavia Tornado	*Paranoia dot van*
Westland Helicopter	*Del wants erotic help*
Rockwell Commander	*Mad wreck moron cell*

ASTRONOMERS & ASTRONOMY

Patrick Moore	*Atomic porker*
John Couch Adams	*Jocund hash coma*
Robert Grant Aiken	*Treating rare knob*
Andromeda	*Adored man*
Big Bang Theory	*Bright gay bone*
Harold Delas Babcock	*Holds ace blackboard*
A Black Hole	*Ha! Coke ball*
William Christie	*I'm a sillier witch*
Eclipse Year	*Easily creep*
The Milky Way	*I weakly myth*
Sandra Moore Faber	*Feared Arab morons*
Robert Earl Jackson	*To bore carnal jerks*
Bernard Lewis Fanaroff	*Fondlers brew an affair*
Julia Margaret Riley	*A lame jury rat girlie*
Galactic Magnetic Field	*Faced gigantic metallic*
Benjamin Apthorp Gould	*Alphabet-jumping donor*
George Ellery Hale	*He really glee ogre*
Halley's Comet	*Smelly hot ace*
Hawking Radiation	*Aha! OK draining wit*
Bertil Lindblad	*Bland libel dirt*
Nuclear Fusion	*Foul insurance*
William Jacob Luyten	*Well-built joy maniac*
Mars Global Surveyor	*Morosely vulgar bars*
The North Star	*The tart's horn*
Fred Lawrence Whipple	*Welfare when crippled*

BANKS & FINANCIAL INSTITUTIONS

Bank Of England	*Bond ankle fan*
Bank Of Ireland	*Inane drab folk*
Royal Bank Of Scotland	*Stank of bloody carnal*
Midland Bank	*Bald mankind*
Baring's Bank	*Rank bin bags*
Ulster Bank	*Sulk banter*
Provident Financial	*In fanatic devil porn*
Nationwide Building Society	*Tiny daunting bowel idiocies*
Lloyds TSB Group	*Sporty bulldogs*
Barclay's Bank	*Bask by carnal*
London Stock Exchange	*No checks on golden tax*
Norwich Union	*I churn on wino*
US Federal Reserve Bank	*Evade berserk funerals*
Llyod's Of London	*Old fondly loons*
Independent Insurance	*Unseen acne-ridden pint*
Alliance And Leicester	*Selected cranial alien*
Abbey National	*Not a alien baby*
Yorkshire Bank	*Rash kinky bore*
Natwest Group	*Outgrew pants*
Britannic Assurance	*Burn satanic arsenic*
Sun Life	*Fun lies*
United Assurance	*Nude sanctuaries*
Scottish Amicable Life	*Loath fascist imbecile*
Prudential Corporation	*Proletarian production*
Commercial Union	*I am moronic uncle*

BATTLES AND WARS

Russian Civil War	*Racial virus wins*
World War One	*No Lewd arrow*
World War Two	*Wow! Lord Wart*
The Vietnam War	*I'm new, have tart!*
The Gulf War	*We hurt flag*
The Battle Of The Boyne	*Ho ho! Bent feeble tatty*
The Falklands War	*What flak slander*
The Cold War	*World cheat*
The Korean War	*Wreak another*
The Great War	*The rage wart*
The American Civil War	*Eh? Active war-criminal*
Battle Of Hastings	*Blatant ego shifts*
The Balkan Wars	*Wash rank table*
The Sea Bering Wars	*Bearings wreathes*
The Boer War	*The rear bow*
The Spanish Civil War	*Whip evil anarchists*
The Pacific War	*Wept if archaic*
Battle Of Britain	*A finite tart blob*
Battle Of The Bulge	*Feeble hot lag butt*
The Indian Border War	*Now harebrained dirt*
The Congo Civil War	*Grown chaotic evil*
Yugoslavia Civil War	*I rag vivacious wally*
The Crimean War	*Na! Warm heretic*
The Yom Kippur War	*Our wimpy park*
The China Border War	*Rich, now threadbare*

CAT BREEDS

Blue Cream Persian	*Mean puerile crabs*
Black Persian	*Spank calibre*
Red Tabby	*Rat by bed*
Tortie Tabby	*It batty bore*
Chocolate Tortie	*Theoretical coot*
Chinchilla	*In chic hall*
Colourpoint Kitten	*Lout kin protection*
Seal Point Birman	*An impersonal bit*
Silver Tabby	*Vilest by bar*
Blue Mitted Ragdoll	*Modelled brutal git*
The Brown Tabby	*Bent wart hobby*
Black Smoke	*Smack bloke*
Red Spotted Manx	*Top sex-mad trend*
Tortoiseshell Cymric	*Smoothly circles tier*
American Wirehair	*Wearier hair manic*
Blue Exotic Shorthair	*Hotter bisexual choir*
Black Silver Ocicat	*Evil cocktail crabs*
Blue Abyssinian	*Ba! I slay bunnies*
Havana Brown	*Ah! Nova brawn*
Snow Bengal	*New slob nag*
White Cornish Rex	*Historic wren hex*
Lilac Point Devon Rex	*Exploit rancid novel*
Black And White Sphynx	*Think bad sex lynch paw*
Sable Burmese	*Resemble a bus*
Brown Ticked Singapura	*I spanking coward brute*

CHARITIES

Children In Need	*Held nice dinner*
National Animal Welfare Trust	*Wasteful international alarm*
Association Of Children's Hospices	*SOS! Chooses arch-fiend politicians*
British Deaf Association	*Hoarse if sad antibiotics*
Comic Relief	*Crime of lice*
Prince's Trust	*Spit currents*
Salvation Army	*Ovary talisman*
Carer's National Association	*Anti-social scenario or Satan!*
Help the Aged	*Get head help*
Children Nationwide	*Ironhanded twin lice*
The Samaritans	*Satanism heart*
Healthlink Worldwide	*Hell! Thank wild weirdo*
Charity Commission	*My comic historians*
National Heart Research Fund	*Non-nuclear trashier fat head*
National Meningitis Fund	*Fine insulting damnation*
Aid For The Aged In Distress	*Retarded oafishness digit*
Caring Cancer Trust	*Cut nicer car grants*
Friends Of The Animals	*Aha! Feminist fondlers*
British Geriatrics Society	*Irritates bitchy ego crisis*
Greensleeves Homes Trust	*The lout germ severeness*
Dogs For The Disabled	*Odd bigoted flashers*
Childline	*Hid in cell*
Child Accident Prevention Trust	*Crap! Ditch volunteered instinct*
Chernobyl Children's Lifeline	*Friendly heroines clinch bill*
Marie Curie Fund	*Unfair rude mice*

CLASSIC CARS

Armstrong Siddeley	*Tiny gormless dread*
Aston Martin Lagonda	*Malignant Satan door*
Camaro SS, Chevrolet	*Molester's havoc car*
Chevette HS, Vauxhall	*Haul velvet sex hatch*
Gordon Keeble	*OK legend bore*
Lamborghini Countach	*Broccoli-hating human*
Impreza Turbo, Subaru	*Barbarize up our smut*
Mitsubishi Space Wagon	*Bigamous pain switches*
Oldsmobile Toronado	*Lobotomies and drool*
Road Runner, Plymouth	*Ultramodern yup horn*
Supra Turbo, Toyota	*Boy! A tortuous trap*
Atlantic, Austin	*Na! A lunatic's tit*
Volkswagen Beetle	*Blast! New geek love*
Willys Overland	*Darn! Lowly evils*
Rover Mini Cooper	*I over price moon*
Lamborghini Espada	*Gosh! Paid lamebrain*
Land Rover Discovery	*Involved racy orders*
Princess Austin	*Niusance strips*
Carrera RS, Porsche	*Crash scrape error*
Peugot Cabriolet	*Apologetic brute*
A-Class Mercedes	*Caressed camels*
Borgward Isabella	*A bad gorilla's brew*
Nissan Skyline	*Ninny likes ass*
Renualt Williams Clio	*Well, is a criminal lout*
Alpine Sunbeam	*Is amenable pun*

DOG BREEDS

Australian Silky Terrier	*Rarity as killer urinates*
Border Terrier	*Er? It bred error*
French Bulldog	*Bled frog lunch*
King Charles Spaniel	*An English-like scrap*
Pomeranian	*Iron Apeman*
German Shephard	*Harsh peg mender*
Rottweiler	*Riot welter*
Yorkshire Terrier	*Sorry hiker, retire!*
American Cocker Spaniel	*Compile skin-cancer area*
Basset Hound	*SOS! Nude bath!*
English Cocker Spaniel	*Hello! Sick Pregnancies*
Jack Russell Terrier	*Jerk's rarer slut lice*
Miniature Poodle	*O! I am politer nude*
Shetland Sheepdog	*Hold deepest gnash*
Staffordshire Bull Terrier	*Hell! Fair first-order brutes*
Bearded Collie	*Old edible race*
Border Collie	*Old lice borer*
Golden Retreiver	*Err..enter evil dog?*
Irish Walter Spaniel	*Is airplane whistler*
Labrador Retriever	*Drab relative error*
Afghan Hound	*Hah! Fun gonad*
Bernese Mountain Dog	*Damn it! Generous bone*
German Pointer	*Prominent rage*
Doberman Pinscher	*Specimen born hard*
Saint Bernard	*An inbred star*

FAIRYTALES & FOLKLORE CHARACTERS

Little Red Riding Hood	*Hitler tried doodling*
The Ugly Duckling	*Yuck! Hell dung git*
The Hare And The Tortoise	*He's rotten to the airhead*
Emperor's New Clothes	*Mere worthless ponce*
Giants of St Michael's Mount	*Oh no! Glummest anti-fascist*
Hansel And Gretel	*Neanderthal legs*
Briar Rose	*Is rear orb*
Maui And The Great Fish	*He is maturing fathead*
The Boy And The Leopard	*Deathbed honey patrol*
Cinderella	*Lid cleaner*
Handsome Prince	*Denser champion*
The Ugly Sisters	*Slithery guests*
Wicked Stepmother	*Mock the weird pest*
The Pied Piper Of Hamelin	*I hated Oppenheimer flip*
The Old Man And His Grandson	*Damn snarling hotheads nod*
A Fish Of The World	*Whore of sad filth*
The Princess And The Pea	*Pint presents headache*
The Princess And The Frog	*Arch-fiend serpent ghost*
The Princess In The Tower	*Represent this in the cow*
Three Raindrops	*A horrid present*
The Day The Sun Hid	*The hashed nudity*
Goldilocks And The Three Bears	*Ho ho! Dredge blackest I latrines*
Rumpilstiltskin	*Insult limp skirt*
Popocatepetl And The Princess	*Elephant postponed practices*
The Nightingale	*He ate lightning*

MOTORBIKES

Ariel Red Hunter	*Rude hen trailer*
Velocette Venom	*One velvet comet*
Scott Flying Squirrel	*Grisly flirt conquest*
Triumph Thunderbird Sport	*Horrid truth stripped numb*
Excelsior Manxman	*Relax! I'm sex con man*
Vincent Black Shadow	*Now vast bald chicken*
Norton Commando	*Moron ant condom*
Harley-Davidson Sturgis	*Horridly savage nudists*
Indian Chief	*Hi! A nice find*
Honda Super Blackbird	*No! Rubs baldhead prick*
Brough Superior	*Ugh! Poor bruiser*
Harley Davidson Electra Glide	*Coldheartedly greased villainy*
Motto Guzzi Le Mans	*Mezzo mating louts*
Garelli Tiger Cross	*Girl regrets social*
Velocette Viceroy	*Icy erect love vote*
Bimota Tesi	*I omit beast*
Rudge Ulster	*Set drug rule*
Henderson Four	*No! On rude flesh*
Honda Monkey	*Man on donkey*
Yamaha Virago	*A hard via yoga*
Honda Superdream	*Rude ashamed porn*
Buell Lightning	*He glinting bull*
Triumph Bonneville	*Virulent phone limb*
Suzuki Bandit	*A dun US kibbutz*
Norton Black Shadow	*Clown's apt handbook*

MYTHS AND LEGENDS

The Minotaur	*I mutant hero*
Brunhild And Sigurd	*Drain lush bird dung*
The Magical Sword	*This large mad cow*
The Knights Of The Round Table	*Thud bleakest hot non-fighter*
Apollo And Daphne	*Append an old halo*
Diana Of Versailles	*Aid favorless alien*
Echo And Narcissus	*SOS! Anarchic nudes*
Psyche And Zephyrus	*Pseud's crazy hyphen*
The Rape Of Helen	*Ho! Free elephant*
The Forge Of Vulcan	*Oh no! Vulgar effect*
Pluto And Proserpina	*I supported anal porn*
Hercules And The Hydra	*Shh! Nude lad treachery*
Perseus And Andromeda	*Dreads darn menopause*
The Triumph Of Galatea	*Amputate the frail hog!*
Flying Mercury	*Fry my gin ulcer*
Medea And Absyrtus	*Surname stayed bad*
Helen On The Walls Of Troy	*Hello! Loathe new Y-fronts*
Danae And The Tower Of Brass	*Na! Farted as worst bone head*
Bellerophon and Anteia	*Non-portable alien head*
The Farnese Bull	*Eh? Fallen brutes*
Varvakeion Statuette	*Eureka! Attain TV votes*
Cupid Asleep	*Spice up deal*
The Return of Persephone	*He's the porn fortune peer*
Ariadne In Naxos	*Sin and anorexia*
Atlanta's Race	*A carnal state*

NEWSPAPERS & MAGAZINES

The Mirror Newspaper	*Prime whore partners*
Cosmopolitan	*Captions loom*
The Guardian	*Huge arid tan*
The Irish News	*Sins herewith*
The Observer	*Severe throb*
The Radio Times	*I am the editors*
The Financial Times	*Nice intimate flash*
Playboy Magazine	*Yo! Big lazy ape-man*
The Sunday Times	*Hey! Nudist mates*
The Sunday Post	*Up the nasty sod*
Fortean Times	*I monster feat*
OK Magazine	*I amaze Kong*
Private Eye	*Pay eerie TV*
Smash Hits	*Hash mists*
Match Football Magazine	*Hello! Amazing fat combat*
Q Music Magazine	*In mega scam quiz*
Vogue Magazine	*Give guano maze*
The TV Times	*Test the vim*
The Evening Standard	*Deviant tender gnash*
The National Enquirer	*Learnt heroin antique*
The Sunday World	*Hey, drowns adult!*
The People	*Hotel peep*
Dreamwatch	*A mad wretch*
The Dark Side	*Dated shriek*
Good Housekeeping	*Go peek in doghouse*

OCEAN DWELLING CREATURES

Pink-Headed Frogfish	*Dope freak finds high*
Great White Shark	*Higher weak tarts*
Long-Finned Eel	*Lone fin legend*
The Dubious Frogfish	*Shh! Fed furious bigot*
Eye Stripe Tigerfish	*Tipsy eerie fighters*
Blue Dolphins	*Posh nude bill*
Killer Whale	*Warlike hell*
Great Blue Whale	*Huge water label*
The Jellyfish	*Hey! Jilt flesh*
Splendid Mandarinfish	*Damn! Darn fiendish lips*
The Common Stinkfish	*Feminist shock month*
Saddled Butterflyfish	*He'd rudest stiff baldly*
Humphead Bannerfish	*Shhh! Rub apeman fiend*
Blotched Hawkfish	*Folks which bathed*
Falcon Hawkfish	*Lank chaos whiff*
The Shark Sucker	*Struck reek hash*
Slender Suckerfish	*Fresh kid cruelness*
Blue Spotted Stingray	*Tatty old Superbeings*
Black Rockfish	*Bricks of chalk*
Smooth Cornetfish	*Christ! Soften homo*
Tasmanian Starfish	*Faint Satanism rash*
Silver Drummer	*Mrs Evil murder*
Spangled Emperor	*Grope damn lepers*
Blacktail Snapper	*Bleak claptrap sin*
Copper Bullseye	*Solely creep pub*

PARTS OF THE BODY

Breasts	*Set bras*
The Digestive Tract	*Straight detective*
Capillaries	*Special liar*
The Diaphragm	*Mad pig hearth*
The Trachea	*Cheat hater*
Wisdom Teeth	*I'm the wet sod*
The Gall Bladder	*Hell! Let dad brag*
Large Intestine	*Entire genitals*
Hair Follicles	*Fear chill soil*
The Stomach	*Ms. Hot cheat*
The Pelvis	*Shelve pit*
The Tricep Muscles	*Cruel chemist pest*
The Fingertips	*Inept fighters*
The Retinas	*This neater*
The Salivary Gland	*Interval lady hags*
Tongue	*Ego nut*
The Spinal Cord	*Posh cretin lad*
Brain Stem	*Tribesman*
Invertebral Discs	*Brainless verdict*
The Thyroid	*Hey! Hot dirt*
Testicles	*Lice tests*
The Ovaries	*Hear soviet*
Ulna and Radius	*And usual drain*
Fallopian Tube	*A pub fellation*
Chromosones	*Oh, cross memo*

PLANTS

Holly Thistle	*The sloth lily*
Wall Germander	*Ram garden well*
Garden Thyme	*The randy gem*
Meadow Sage	*O! Mad sewage*
The Dandelion	*Hand deletion*
The Wild Orchid	*Weird hot child*
Sea Buckthorn	*Sunbathe rock*
Black Helleborne	*A lech blob kernel*
Cornelian Cherry	*Near horny circle*
White Dead Nettle	*Wanted — idle teeth*
Common Buckthorn	*Rock-bottom men hunch*
Castor Oil Plant	*Pollinators act*
Spindle Tree	*Idle serpent*
Yellow Foxglove	*Well, go foxy love!*
Lily Of The Valley	*Lovely thief ally*
Mistletoe	*Me toilets*
Iceland Moss	*I demon class*
Wild Pansy	*Windy pals*
Hart's Tongue Fern	*Fatso hen grunter*
Passion Flower	*Now SAS profile*
Cherry Laurel	*Rural lechery*
Cow Parsnip	*Now sip carp*
Waterlily	*Tire wally*
Deadly Nightshade	*Dangle dishy death*
Opium Poppy	*You pop pimp*

PROFESSIONS

Computer Programmer	*Mature germ romp crop*
Clerical Officer	*Lice frolic farce*
University Professor	*Serious viper Y-fronts*
School Teacher	*Cheers! Loo chat*
Graphic Designer	*Rigid gnash creep*
Newspaper Journalist	*O Jesus! Nipple warrant*
Features Editor	*Diet of treasure*
Library Assistant	*Slays brain artist*
Professional Musician	*In famous lips scenario*
Professional Footballer	*Laboratories on off spell*
Data Analyst	*Ta, Lady Satan*
Hotel Manager	*The lame groan*
Brain Surgeon	*Boring a nurse*
Funeral Director	*Fornicated ruler*
Health Visitor	*This vital hero*
Dental Technician	*A lichen-tinted can*
Pharmacy Technician	*I'm acne anarchy pitch*
Ladies' Hairdresser	*Dire idle harassers*
Prison Warden	*Inward person*
Police Officer	*Epic foe frolic*
Production Worker	*Now root rude prick*
Television Presenter	*Elite net perversions*
Motor Mechanic	*A commoner itch*
Bar Manager	*Man barrage*
Defence Lawyer	*Free weedy clan*

SPECIES OF BIRD

Peachfaced Lovebird	*Fabled divorcee chap*
Red Factor Canary	*A fancy rat record*
Masked Lovebird	*Drive blokes mad*
Mealy Amazon Parrot	*A rampant lazy Romeo*
Albino Budgerigar	*A drab religion bug*
Dark Green Budgerigar	*Eager bigger drunkard*
Lutino Cocktail	*Cool lunatic kit*
Blue Lovebird	*Rude evil blob*
Fischer's Lovebird	*Cold feverish ribs*
Senegal Parrot	*Strangle opera*
Red Bellied Parrot	*Terrible odder pal*
Blue Fronted Amazon	*Fundamental boozer*
Maximilian's Parrot	*Mix animal's airport*
Green Winged Macaw	*Menacing war wedge*
Red Masked Conure	*OK dunce dreamers*
Maroon Bellied Conure	*Loonier demon curable*
Ring Necked Parakeet	*Kick renegade parent*
Moluccan Cockatoo	*Onto Coca-Cola muck*
Roseate Cockatoo	*Coo! Coo! Seek a tart*
Green Naped Lorikeet	*Dire teenage plonker*
Greater Hill Mynah	*Large alien rhythm*
Yorkshire Canary	*A risky horny race*
Domestic Canary	*Mayor's accident*
Bengalese Finch	*Single, hence fab*
Lutino Budgerigar	*Original drug tube*

HIT 1970s SONGS

The Wonder of You	*You whored often*
Close To You	*Yo! Cute loos*
I Hear You Knocking	*Ouch, kinkier agony*
My Sweet Lord	*Try some lewd*
Anarchy In The UK	*Hairy nuke chant*
Amazing Grace	*Camera gazing*
School's Out	*Cool shouts*
Lean On Me	*Men on ale*
I Can See Clearly Now	*A! Encores! Nice wally*
Long Haired Lover From Liverpool	*Hello! Diploma of revolving error*
Cum On Feel The Noise	*Lonesome chief tune*
I'm The Leader of the Gang (I am)	*Oh dear me! I am a gentle fight*
Live and Let Die	*Devil dateline*
Let's Get it On	*Lent egotist*
Seasons In The Sun	*Sunshine as tones*
Waterloo	*Loo water*
Kung Fu Fighting	*Huffing gut king*
Bohemian Rhapsody	*Ha ha! Spy in bedroom*
Space Oddity	*Acid type sod*
Don't Go Breaking My Heart	*OK mad rent-boy gathering*
Mull Of Kintyre	*Oh my! Full tinker*
Stayin' Alive	*A evil sanity*
Rivers of Babylon	*Snobbery of rival*
I Will Survive	*View ill virus*
Bright Eyes	*Eh? Grey bits!*

HIT 1980s SONGS

Do They Know It's Christmas?	*This whacked monstrosity*
Blue Monday	*Bemoan duly*
In The Air Tonight	*Retaining hot hit*
If I Could Turn Back Time	*Doubtful I'm a nice trick*
Ride On Time	*I'm dire tone*
I Just Called To Say I Love You	*Let us joyously violate acid*
Another Day In Paradise	*Oh dear! insanity parade*
Every Breath You Take	*Hey! Above-rate turkey*
Cat Among The Pigeons	*On egotist champagne*
Sowing The Seeds Of Love	*Goodness of the weevils*
Ebony And Ivory	*Vain boy yonder*
Super Trouper	*Pore ruptures*
Tainted Love	*Violent date*
Golden Brown	*Wrong blonde*
The Birdie Song	*Bigoted shrine*
Kids In America	*I'm in a sick read*
Baggy Trousers	*Robust grey gas*
Babooshka	*Shook ABBA*
Dancing In The Street	*Nice stringent death*
Take On Me	*Amok teen*
Brass In Pocket	*Broken spastic*
La Isla Bonita	*Boil Alsatian*
The Only Way is Up	*Hey you! Want lips?*
Don't Worry Be Happy	*Worthy brandy pope*
Eternal Flame	*Female rental*

HIT 1960S ALBUMS

Abbey Road	*Bad boy era*
The Freewhelin' Bob Dylan	*Redefine new healthy blob*
All Summer Long	*Small loner mug*
Rubber Soul	*Sour rubble*
Sounds Of Silence	*'e fondles cousins*
Blonde On Blonde	*Boned bonne doll*
Younger Than Yesterday	*Starry-eyed naughty one*
The Piper At The Gates Of Dawn	*Grow fattened hash appetite*
Ogden's Nut Gone Flake	*OK... engage nuts fondle*
Wheels Of Fire	*Wife hole serf*
Waiting For The Sun	*Now huge if in tarts*
Electric Ladyland	*Cancelled dirt lay*
The Village Green Preservation Society	*Essentially interpretive hog coverage*
Beggars Banquet	*Request bag bang*
Dusty In Memphis	*This dummy spine*
With A Little Help From My Friends	*Hmm! Filthily filtered sworn tape*
Everybody Knows This Is Nowhere	*Oh Wow! Everybody's inherent kiss*
Aretha's Gold	*Lad shortage*
Trout Mask Replica	*Proletariat's muck*
In The Court Of The Crimson King	*Hoho! Reminscent fork cutting*
Let It Bleed	*Be little ed*
Who Knows Where The Time Goes	*Oh Wow! Get this new meek horse*
Hollies Greatest	*Let shortages lie*
Super Session	*Person issues*
Sweetheart At The Rodeo	*To a hotter heated sewer*

FEMALE POPSTARS OF THE 1960s

Diana Ross	*O! Ass drain*
Dusty Springfield	*If disgruntled spy*
Nancy Sinatra	*A racist nanny*
Brenda Lee	*Ale bender*
Petula Clark	*Lack true pal*
Miss Cilla Black	*Cabs claim kills*
Connie Francis	*Financiers' con*
Aretha Franklin	*Hark, latrine fan*
Miss Jeanne Black	*Blanks jane's mice*
Dinah Washington	*Shh! Not wind again!*
Shirley Bassey	*Eh? Barely sissy!*
Anita Bryant	*A natty brain*
Anne Shelton	*Hates Lennon*
Linda Scott	*Sold intact*
Doris Day	*I do yards*
Miss Janis Joplin	*Sin joins lips jam*
Mary Wells	*Wary smell*
Peggy Lee	*Leggy pee*
Brenda Holloway	*Oh! Now really bad*
Sandie Shaw	*Win ass-head*
Anita Harris	*A hair strain*
Miss Gladys Knight	*Smith's gangly kids*
Dionne Warwick	*Wow! Nice in dark*
Nina Simone	*No! I'm insane!*
Mary Hopkin	*Him porky? Na!*

MALE POPSTARS OF THE 1960s

Bob Dylan	*Bland boy*
Paul Mc Cartney	*Pay 'Mr Clean Cut'*
Richard Starkey	*Rather scary kid*
George Harrison	*Ogreish groaner*
Elvis Presley	*Yes, serve pill*
Mister Jim Morrison	*I'm mirror joint mess*
James Brown	*Mr Jawbones*
Stevie Wonder	*Weirdo events*
Otis Redding	*Stoned rigid*
Louis Armstrong	*A monstrous girl*
Scott Walker	*Total wrecks*
Billy Preston	*Rent-boy pills*
Val Doonican	*An avid colon*
Mr Gene Pitney	*Rent enemy pig*
Mr Roy Orbison	*Yo! Mirror snob*
Frank Sinatra	*A far ran stink*
Mister Cliff Richard	*Terrific child farms*
Marvin Gaye	*My! In a grave*
Roger Miller	*Grime roller*
Burt Bacharach	*Hurrah! A BBC act!*
Chuck Berry	*Buck her cry*
Georgie Fame	*Mega ego fire*
Jim Reeves	*Mere jives*
Billy J. Kramer	*My ill bra jerk*
Nat King Cole	*Lacking tone*

POP & ROCK BANDS OF THE 1960S

The Beatles	*The best ale*
The Rolling Stones	*Hello! Snorting set*
Procul Harum	*Parlour chum*
The Shangri-La's	*Hash triangles*
The Animals	*I'm the nasal*
The Temptations	*This potent meat*
The Dave Clark Five	*Ha! Feel dick rave*
The Foundations	*Oh no! Fats United!*
Supremes	*Pure mess*
Peter And Gordon	*Deranged to porn*
The Walker Brothers	*Rat blokes threw her*
The Mamas and The Papas	*Stamp mean paths ahead*
Simon and Garfunkel	*Engulf anorak minds*
The Small Faces	*Smell fat aches*
The Yardbirds	*Dirty bed rash*
The Beach Boys	*Hey! Bob cheats!*
The Four Seasons	*Unsafe shooters*
The Velvet Underground	*Thunder love drug event*
Freddie and The Dreamers	*Retarded arse! Defend him!*
The Everly Brothers	*They brothel server*
The Righteous Brothers	*Heigh-ho! Sober strutter*
Gerry and The Pacemakers	*My Carp! Degenerate shark!*
The Seekers	*Sheet reeks!*
The Ronettes	*On the street*
Martha and The Vandellas	*Ha! Lamented trash vandal*

HIT ALBUMS OF THE 1970S

Toys In The Attic	*The station city*
Every Picture Tells A Story	*Totally perverse security*
Exile On Main Street	*Into alien extremes*
London Calling	*Loon land cling*
Layla And Other Assorted Love Songs	*Total asshead and over glossy loner*
Ray Charles Live	*Silvary lecher*
Tonight's The Night	*Shhh! Getting on tit!*
Let's Get It On	*O! Gentle tits*
Where There's Smoke	*Eh? Seek whore terms*
More Song About Buildings And Roads	*Underdog Australians good snobbism*
Garvey's Ghost	*Shaggy voters*
Paradise And Lunch	*An underpaid clash*
Unknown Pleasures	*Unspoken rune laws*
Hank Williams Jr And Friends	*Finish small and inward jerk*
Everything You Know Is Wrong	*Oh wow! Envy striking younger*
Off The Wall	*Who fell flat*
The Rise And Fall Of Ziggy Stardust	*Zonally frigid daughters fastest*
Heat Treatment	*Mean teeth tart*
The Complete Buddy Holly	*O hell! Botchy type muddle*
Alive On Arrival	*O, an evil arrival*
Plastic Ono Band	*Old Captain Snob*
Hearts Of Stone	*Fat heroes' snot*
Meaty, Beaty, Big And Bouncy	*Bogey baby cyanide mutant*
Darkness On The Edge Of Town	*Shh! A stoned forgotten weekend*
Plastic Letters	*Spectral titles*

FEMALE POPSTARS OF THE 1970S

Carly Simon	*Moan lyrics*
Gloria Gayner	*Ay! Large groin!*
Marie Osmond	*Mormon ideas*
Carole King	*OK girl acne*
Joan Baez	*A zone jab*
Melanie	*Mean Lie*
Roberta Flack	*Brat rock flea*
Ann-Marie David	*Darn! Vain media*
Miss Suzi Quatro	*Quiz us amorists*
Vicki Lawrence	*Evil wine crack*
Karen Carpenter	*A percent ranker*
Lynsey De Paul	*Slyly nude ape*
Debby Boone	*Boy be on bed*
Olivia Newton-John	*Ha! Now in joint love*
Miss Helen Reddy	*Hey! Sins meddler*
Donna Summer	*Damn sour men!*
Maria Muldaur	*I am aural drum*
Joni Mitchell	*Hmm! Joins lice list*
Stephanie De Sykes	*The pissed Yankees*
Minnie Riperton	*I emit inner porn*
Tammy Wynette	*My! My! A wet tent*
Maxine Nightingale	*Ha! Negligent in exam*
Bonnie Tyler	*Rent-boy line*
Julie Covington	*Not loving juice*
Elkie Brooks	*OK bloke rise*

MALE POPSTARS OF THE 1970S

Eric Clapton	*Narcoleptic*
Barry Manilow	*Library woman*
David Essex	*Sex advised*
Donald Clark Osmond	*Damn old lads on rock*
Gary Glitter	*Target girly*
Richard Clayderman	*Rancid lady charmer*
Rod Stewart	*Rated worst*
Steven Tyler	*Svelte entry*
Gilbert O' Sullivan	*Isn't globular evil!*
Neil Diamond	*I'm dandelion*
David Bowie	*I vow baddie*
Bill Withers	*Is web thrill*
Mister Johnny Nash	*Shh! Remnant sin joy*
Little Jimmy Osmond	*Jolly timid moments*
Jermaine Jackson	*Join man jerks ace*
Alvin Stardust	*Valid nuts star*
Alice Cooper	*Oi! Coal creep!*
Charlie Rich	*Her chic liar*
Mr Cat Stevens	*Mass TV centre*
Barry White	*Wiry breath*
Carl Douglas	*Drugs a local*
Neil Sedaka	*Ideal snake*
James Taylor	*Oral majesty*
Frankie Vallie	*Evil nail freak*
Roger Whittaker	*Grew OK tart heir*

POP & ROCK BANDS OF THE 1970S

Aerosmith	*Hire atoms*
The Jackson Five	*Fetch vain jokes*
Free	*Reef*
Fleetwood Mac	*O! Welcomed fat*
Hot Chocolate	*Cool hot cheat*
Deep Purple	*Upped leper*
The Carpenters	*Pretence trash*
The Osmonds	*Shot demons*
Atomic Rooster	*I resort to coma*
The Chi-Lites	*Lithe ethics*
Mott The Hoople	*O! Hotpot helmet*
The Miracles	*Rich lame set*
The Moody Blues	*Eh? Embody louts*
The Eagles	*He gets ale*
Rhythm Heritage	*My! The higher lout*
Stylistics	*I list cysts*
Brotherhood Of Man	*Bathroom fond hero*
The Doobie Brothers	*Ho ho! Bore bedsitter*
Detroit Spinners	*Porn disinterest*
Earth, Wind and Fire	*Fine inward hatred*
The Bay City Rollers	*Tolerably hysteric!*
The Steve Miller Band	*Hell! Bed-time servant*
Three Degrees	*He reset greed*
Average White Band	*A heaving water-bed*
KC and The Sunshine Band	*Enhanced husband stink*

FEMALE POPSTARS OF THE 1980S

Madonna Louise Ciccone	*Occasional nude income*
Miss Kim Wilde	*Kid slime swim*
Elaine Page	*Ape lineage*
Kim Carnes	*Skin cream*
Sheena Easton	*Aha! Tone sense*
Toni Basil	*Is ant boil*
Laura Branigan	*Na! Grab a urinal*
Tina Turner	*Errant unit*
Debbie Gibson	*Is big bed bone*
Tracey Chapman	*Pay man-catcher*
Cyndi Lauper	*Lunacy pride*
Alison Moyet	*Oh my! Toe-nails!*
Hazell Dean	*Na! Hell daze*
Mica Paris	*I scam pair*
Barbara Dickson	*Bad brain croaks*
Suzanne Vega	*Save nun gaze*
Kate Bush	*Shake but!*
Whitney Houston	*Ho ho! Nutty swine*
Miss Jennifer Rush	*Jesus firm her sin'n*
Anita Baker	*A bra intake*
Belinda Carlisle	*Illiberal dances*
Sarah Brightman	*Margin hash brat*
Debbie Harry	*A hybrid beer*
Kylie Minogue	*I like 'em young*
Gloria Estefan	*Large fat noise*

MALE POPSTARS OF THE 1980S

Bruce Springsteen	*Epic beers 'n' grunts*
Chris Rea	*Rich arse*
George Michael	*I come, he gargle!*
Meat Loaf	*O,fat male!*
Michael Bolton	*I'm the local nob*
The Artist formerly known as Prince	*'Hen's wife' rocker rants importantly*
Rick Astley	*Tick-slayer*
Axl Rose	*Oral sex*
Mister Kenny Rogers	*Grr! So enemy stinker*
Phil Collins	*Ill inch slop*
Peter Gabriel	*Glib repartee*
Shakin' Stevens	*Heavens! Stinks*
Julio Iglesias	*Oi! ugliness jail*
Christopher Cross	*Hip-scorcher sorts*
Michael Jackson	*Hijack on camel*
Captain Sensible	*Cannabis epistle*
Lionel Richie	*I'll ice heroin*
Billy Joel	*Jolly bile*
Bob Marley	*My! Ear blob*
Paul Young	*Na! You gulp!*
Billy Ocean	*On icy label*
Mr Howard Jones	*Moron jaws herd*
Mister Jason Donovan	*Damn! Join on overt ass*
Mister Richard Marx	*Drat! Richer Marxism*
Terence Trent D'Arby	*Battery centre nerd*

POP & ROCK BANDS OF THE 1980S

Dexy's Midnight Runners	*Hundreds try sex-mining*
Joy Division	*I void sin joy*
Village People	*Agile level pop*
Bad Manners	*Na! Mend bras*
Adam and The Ants	*Damn Satan death!*
Madness	*Mend ass*
Spandau Ballet	*Bad as null tape*
Transvision Vamp	*In vast vain romps*
Talking Heads	*Na! The kid lags*
The Stray Cats	*She acts tarty*
Frankie Goes To Hollywood	*Howl to foresaken ideology*
Fun Boy Three	*Hey, rub often!*
The Pointer Sisters	*O! It represents this*
The Human League	*Ha! Huge male tune*
Dire Straits	*Art is direst*
Tears For Fears	*Safe fat errors*
Eurythmics	*My hit cures*
Echo and The Bunnymen	*Beyond tune henchman*
Air Supply	*Slip up ray*
Depeche Mode	*He'd come deep*
Bananarama	*Ram a banana*
Siouxsie and The Banshees	*Shh! Nauseate inside boxes*
Fine Young Cannibals	*No! Nicely abusing fan*
Crowded House	*Ouch! Odd sewer*
Everything But The Girl	*Grr! Hit the evil bent guy*

HIT ALBUMS OF THE 1980S

King Of America	*I reckon I'm a fag*
Dig Your Own Hole	*Oh no! Ugly weirdo!*
Sticky Fingers	*Sic frisky gent*
Script Of A Jester's Tear	*Spare reject of artists*
Sign O' The Times	*This tone is gem*
Strong Persuader	*Sad poser grunter*
The Jackie Wilson Story	*Wonky halitosis reject*
On The Boardwalk	*Weak harlot bond*
Searching For The Young Soul Rebels	*Lecherous gangrenous filthy bores*
Speak And Spell	*'Spank!' lad pleas*
Hysteria	*This year*
No Jacket Required	*Acquired jerk tone*
Hunting High And Low	*Huh! Now dangling hit*
Stay On These Roads	*Yeah! Rotten as sods*
Prince Charming	*Enriching cramp*
Appetite For Destruction	*Dire, fat prostitute ponce*
Welcome To The Beautiful South	*Automobile fleets chew hut out*
Limping For A Generation	*Filtering egomania porn*
The Age Of Consent	*Gosh! Not acne feet!*
Hounds Of Love	*Sound of hovel*
Michael Jackson's Thriller	*Kill slash harmonic reject*
Like A Virgin	*A virile king*
Colour By Numbers	*Ole! Bury born scum*
Sweet Dreams	*Weed masters*
Be Yourself Tonight	*Glory be of this tune*

FEMALE POPSTARS OF THE 1990S

Mariah Carey	*A creamy hair*
Shania Twain	*Aha! I win Satan*
Lauryn Hill	*Any ill hurl*
Britney Spears	*I present brays*
Celine Dion	*No! I decline*
Courtney Love	*Very cool tune*
Sheryl Crow	*Her slow cry*
Sinead O'Connor	*Do insane croon*
Ms Mary J. Blige	*Jammy gerbils!*
Geri Halliwell	*Girlie hell law*
Victoria Adams	*O! Dramatic visa*
Shirley Manson	*Snarls "I'm honey"*
Vanessa Paradis	*Parades vain ass*
Lisa Stansfield	*Is fallen sadist*
Gabrielle	*Libel rage*
Dina Carroll	*I carnal lord*
Michelle Gayle	*Heal my leg lice*
Toni Braxton	*Tart in box? No!*
Alannah Myles	*Na! Small hyena*
Maria McKee	*Cake maimer*
Kim Appleby	*Peaky blimp*
Cathy Dennis	*Handy insect*
Oleta Adams	*Lo! A sad mate*
Ms Beverley Craven	*Scream verb evenly*
Alanis Morissette	*Snot materialises*

MALE POPSTARS OF THE 1990S

Marti Pellow	*Ill tapeworm*
Peter Andre	*A pretender*
Thom Yorke	*OK to rhyme*
Jarvis Cocker	*Vice rocks raj*
Liam Gallagher	*Ha! Illegal gram*
Damon Albarn	*Na! Moral band*
Fatboy Slim	*Mob falsity*
Bryan Adams	*Drab as many*
Gary Barlow	*Glow ray bra*
Mark Owen	*Woman ark*
Robbie Williams	*I'm a risible blow*
Ronan Keating	*Na! Groin taken*
Kurt Cobain	*OK, cut brain*
Mr Jon Secada	*Major dances*
Mister Bobby Brown	*Bribery bombs town*
Ricky Martin	*My nitric arc*
Edward Barton	*A drowned brat*
Mr Will Smith	*Hmm! Ill wrist*
Michael Stipe	*Slime pit ache*
USA star Frank Black	*Ba! Rascal skunk fart!*
Crispian Mills	*Criminal's lips*
Brett Anderson	*Bender, no tarts!*
Marilyn Manson	*Immoral nannys*
Lenny Kravitz	*Zany TV relink*
Simon Fowler	*Mr Swine fool*

POP & ROCK BANDS OF THE 1990S

The Spice Girls	*Crisis! Get help!*
Ace of Base	*Boa Faeces*
Supergrass	*Spurs rages*
New Kids On The Block	*Now kicks the blonde*
Red Hot Chilli Peppers	*Polish crippled three*
Stereophonics	*Honest copiers*
The Charlatans	*The anal charts*
The Stone Roses	*Thee snot sores*
Wilson Phillips	*Won his lip pills*
The Beautiful South	*The fatuous blue hit*
Garbage	*Rage bag*
The Manic Street Preachers	*Smarter, three piece snatch!*
The Proclaimers	*Recompile trash*
Technotronic	*No hit concert*
Radiohead	*O! A die-hard*
Right Said Fred	*This fried drag*
Color Me Badd	*Boredom clad*
The Divine Comedy	*Hey! Dent dim voice*
The New Power Generation	*Penetrating nowhere! Woe!*
The Wonder Stuff	*He'd wet turn-offs*
Shakespeare's Sister	*Heiresses park seats*
Carter-Unstoppable Sex Machine	*Pubescent Harper's exclamations*
Arrested Development	*Oh man! Deleted perverts*
The Spin Doctors	*Cornish test pod*
The Prodigy	*Pity her dog*

HIT ALBUMS FROM THE 1990S

Pills 'N' Thrills And Bellyaches	*Child brainlessly plants hell*
Ladies And Gentlemen	*Damn! Needle genitals!*
Get A Grip	*Great Pig*
The Beatles Anthology	*Oh hell! Batty stone-age*
Achtung Baby	*A naughty BBC*
Take That And Party	*A hated tatty prank*
Dangerous	*Sound rage*
Live Your Life Be Free	*Yo! Evil eerie bluffer*
The Language Of Life	*Ghoul-eaten fig-leaf*
Walking Wounded	*Now dud weakling*
Nevermind	*Driven men*
Use Your Illusion	*Lousy ruinous lie*
History, Past, Present And Future	*Untrusty person farted this ape*
Different Class	*Endless traffic*
The Great Escape	*Erect stage heap*
Come On Feel The Lemonheads	*He echoed semen fool lament*
What's The Story Morning Glory	*Ole! Lam, end-of-month cheese*
Jagged Little Pill	*Jilted piglet gall*
Emancipation	*I am pint ocean*
The Best Of New Order	*Fettered snob whore*
Chaos And Disorder	*Hardcore as odd sin*
Under The Pink	*Nuked her pint*
Out Of Time	*To emit UFO*
Good News From The Next World	*Extend strong flow whoredom*
Ten Summoner's Tales	*A restless monument*

BEATLES SONGS

Can't Buy Me Love	*Locate bum envy*
Strawberry Fields Forever	*Fewer drivers fart soberly*
Nowhere Man	*No new harem*
She Loves You	*Yo! Use shovel!*
Lucy In The Sky With Diamonds	*Discontinue wild shaky myth*
Yellow Submarine	*Mean lowly bruise*
Paperback Writer	*Beware! Part prick!*
Yesterday	*A seedy try*
A Hard Day's Night	*Had hasty daring*
And I Love Her	*Overlaid hen*
I Wanna Hold Your Hand	*Ha ha! Noddy won urinal!*
Eight Days A Week	*Aged whiskey tea*
All You Need Is Love	*A loosely evil nude*
Eleanor Rigby	*Grr! Obey alien!*
Lady Madonna	*Annoy mad lad*
Ticket To Ride	*I detector kit*
The Long And Winding Road	*Oh! Weird and dangling ton!*
Magical Mystery Tour	*I'm a clumsy tarty ogre*
Hello Goodbye	*Old bogey hole*
Ballad Of John And Yoko	*Fold 'anal joy' handbook*
Come Together	*Go cheer totem*
Day Tripper	*Try dire pap*
Tomorrow Never Knows	*Now, over-work monster*
We Can Work It Out	*Outwit crank? Woe.*
She's A Woman	*Ahem! Won ass*

HIT SONGS OF THE 1960S

Glad All Over	*Lad lover lag*
Flowers In The Rain	*It's infernal whore*
Summer Holiday	*Oh my! Rude mails!*
Return To Sender	*Sure! Rent rodent*
Please Mr Postman	*Meanest romp pals*
Only The Lonely	*Loony yell then*
Are You Lonesome Tonight?	*Reunite moose anthology*
Wonderful Land	*Fall down nuder*
I Remember You	*O my! Eerier bum!*
It's Now Or Never	*Inventor swore*
Cathy's Clown	*Sly cow chant*
You've Lost That Loving Feeling	*Flouting velvety anthologies*
Green Green Grass Of Home	*Heroes of gangrene germs*
Tossin' And Turnin	*No! Nudist sin rant*
Sympathy For The Devil	*Filthy poverty shamed*
I Heard It Through The Grapevine	*Hurrah! degenerative hot pig hit*
It's Not Unusual	*Soul's tuna unit*
I Can't Get No Satisfaction	*Contains fanatic egotist*
A Groovy Kind Of Love	*Forgive loony vodka*
Strangers In The Night	*Ha! Inserting strength*
Reach Out And I'll Be There	*That lonelier debaucher*
Puppet On A String	*Pup spat nitrogen*
A Whiter Shade Of Pale	*Foreheads awat help*
Light My Fire	*Filthy grime*
Daydream Believer	*My! I revealed beard*

HIT 1990S SONGS

Smells Like Teen Spirit	*Termite's penile skills*
Nothing Compares To You	*Hey! I'm not a poetry song*
It Must Have Been Love	*Behave! Most vile tune*
Common People	*Pop clone memo*
Show Me Heaven	*He shave women*
Do The Bartman	*Bad throat men*
(Everything I Do) I Do It For You	*Yo! Oddity or heroin fugitive?*
Heart-shaped box	*X-rated bash hope*
Black Or White	*OK! I blew chart!*
Re-light My Fire	*I'm rightly free*
All That She Wants	*Wasn't health salt*
Sleeping Satellites	*Settle pleasing lies*
My Heart Will Go On	*Oily anthem growl*
Sweet Like Chocolate	*Eh? Satellite coke cow*
Things Can Only Get Better	*Neglecting snotty breath*
Don't Want To Miss A Thing	*Damn it! It wasn't hot song*
Get Ready For This	*Destroy a fighter*
Believe	*Evil bee*
Country House	*Curse on youth*
Parklife	*Lip freak*
Last Train To Trancentral	*Transatlantic loner tart*
Roll With It	*I'll throw it!*
What Time Is Love?	*I'm soviet wealth*
Stupid Girl	*Is dirt plug*
Free As A Bird	*Erase if drab*
World In Motion	*Now on mild riot*

JAZZ MUSICIANS

Courtney Pine	*Puny erection*
Ray Charles	*Archly sear*
Duke Ellington	*Dog-like tunnel*
Thelonious Monk	*OK on loutish men*
John Surman	*Un-jam horns*
Terence Blanchard	*Drench tabernacle*
Herbie Hancock	*Been choir hack*
Keith Jarrett	*The jerk trait*
Louis Armstrong	*A monstrous girl*
Roy Eldridge	*I greedy lord*
Wynton Marsalis	*In womanly stars*
Coleman Hawkins	*New shock animal*
Stan Tracey	*Tyrant case*
Ornette Coleman	*No! Not erect male*
Stephane Grappelli	*Aghast! Nipple leper*
Humphrey Lyttelton	*Oh hell! My pretty nut*
Jan Garbarek	*Nag a bar jerk*
Tony Williams	*It silly woman!*
Charles Mingus	*Ugliness charm*
Toots Thielemans	*Smoothie talents*
Michael Portal	*Ho! All-time carp*
Curtis Counce	*Cute sin occur*
Walt Dickerson	*Cow lad stinker*
Wayne Shorter	*No! Heresy wart*
Lem Winchester	*Slim when erect*
Hank Mobley	*Monkey blah*

RADIO 1 & 2 DISC JOCKEYS

Clive Warren	*Ran evil crew*
Mark Radcliffe	*Farm dick flare*
Marc 'Lard' Riley	*Merry arid call*
Simon Mayo	*Noisy ammo*
Jo Whiley	*I jowly, eh?*
Brian Matthew	*Ambient wrath*
Kevin Greening	*Veneering king*
Robin Boyle	*Bribe loony*
Andy Kershaw	*Shady wanker*
Mary Anne Hobbs	*Ha! Man snobbery*
Pete Tong	*Poet gent*
Tim Westwood	*Wow! Tits demo*
Annie Nightingale	*Annihilating gene*
Dave Pearce	*A deep crave*
Mark Goodyear	*More Okay drag*
Claire Sturgess	*Cruel as tigress*
Trevor Nelson	*No stern lover*
Danny Rampling	*Limp drag nanny*
Chris Goldfinger	*Rich gig fondlers*
Stuart Maconie	*I coarse mutant*
Steve Wright	*Tight swerve*
Alan Keith	*I thank ale*
Humphrey Lyttleton	*Utterly nymph hotel*
Jim Lloyd	*Jolly dim*
David Allan	*Laid vandal*

AMERICAN HISTORICAL FIGURES

General Custer	*Cruel sergeant*
Franklin Pearce	*Infernal packer*
Martin Van Buren	*Vain numb ranter*
Franklin D. Roosevelt	*Find love-lorn streak*
Benjamin Franklin	*Flank inner jib man*
George Washington	*Groaning sweet hog*
John Adams	*Son had jam*
Thomas Jefferson	*man's offshore jet*
James Madison	*I jam demon ass*
Neil Armstrong	*Snort malinger*
Mister 'Buzz' Aldrin	*Blizzard terminus*
James Monroe	*More nose jam*
President John Quincy Adams	*Damndest chap joins enquiry*
President Andrew Jackson	*Renowned and spastic jerk*
William Harrison	*Raw oral nihilism*
John Tyler	*Jolt Henry*
President James Knox Polk	*Old jerk's spank exemption*
Zachary Taylor	*A crazy holy rat*
Millard Fillmore	*I'm real droll film*
James Buchanan	*Human acne jabs*
Abraham Lincoln	*Oh man! An ill crab*
James Garfield	*Jail germs fade*
Benjamin Harrison	*Ha! Bin major sinner*
Theodore Roosevelt	*Sheer voodoo letter*
Herbert Hoover	*Her TV hero bore*

ASSASSINATED & MURDERED FIGURES

Rajiv Gandhi	*Diving rajah*
Itzhak Rabin	*Ah, ran kibitz*
Ngo Dinh Diem	*Hiding demon*
Indira Gandhi	*Hi! Grand India*
Abraham Lincoln	*Hall-born maniac*
Anwar Sadat	*Satan award*
St Thomas a Becket	*Battiest macho sneak*
William of Orange	*I am a regional fowl*
Jean Paul Marat	*Am natural jape*
Spencer Perceval	*Snap clever creep*
James Garfield	*Jeer if mad slag*
Peter Stolypin	*Not tipsy leper*
Michael Collins	*Comical sin hell*
Leon Trotsky	*Knotty loser*
Benito Mussolini	*I'm loonies but sin*
Martin Luther King	*Ugh! Tart in Kremlin*
Salvador Allende	*A landlord leaves*
Olof Palme	*Ample fool*
Bachir Gemayel	*Hereby magical*
Sadi Carnot	*Satanic rod*
Maurice Bishop	*I ambush copier*
General Mohammea Zia ul-Haq	*Ah! Amazing queer llama home*
Ranasinghe Premadasa	*Harassed ape-man grain*
General Raphael Trujillo	*Hell! Injure a large patrol*
Senator Robert Kennedy	*Entered sorry banknote*

BRITISH HISTORICAL FIGURES

Sir Thomas More	*I'm morose trash*
Admiral Nelson	*Mainland loser*
David Lloyd George	*Loyal dog diverged*
Cardinal Wolsey	*Cowardly aliens*
Sir Robert Walpole	*Terrible poor laws*
Spencer Compton	*Con-men prospect*
William Cavendish	*Na! Whimsical devil*
George Greenville	*Reveling ogre glee*
William Pitt	*Law limit tip*
Augustus Henry Fitzroy	*Unfussy hazy tiger rout*
Henry Addington	*Darned tinny hog*
William Wyndham	*Damn! I wally whim*
Spencer Perceval	*Snap clever creep*
Robert Jenkinson	*No! Inert snob jerk*
Frederick Robinson	*Enforces biro drink*
Charles Grey	*Lechery rags*
William Lamb	*Maim law bill*
Sir Robert Peel	*Terrible poser*
Edward Stanley	*Darn sweet lady*
General George Gordon	*Engage logged-on error*
Henry Temple	*Thy leper men*
Benjamin Disraeli	*I'm dense brain jail*
William Gladstone	*Slim giant allowed*
Archibald Primrose	*I'm sad horrible carp*
Arthur Balfour	*Rub a harlot fur*

CHEFS AND COOKS

Delia Smith	*Hate is mild*
Rick Stein	*Nice skirt*
Sally Clarke	*Really slack*
Rose Gray	*Sorry age*
Anthony Worall Thompson	*Na! Now small horny hotpot*
Stephen Bull	*Hell-bent pus*
Adam Robinson	*O man! Arid snob*
Rowley Leigh	*Eh? I orgy well*
Stephen Markwick	*The knacker's wimp*
Christopher Chown	*Shhh! Cow cretin pro*
Carole Evans	*Acne? A solver*
Tessa Bramley	*Measly breast*
Paul Heathcote	*Hate cheap lout*
Terence Laybourne	*Na! Cruel teeny bore*
Paul Rankin	*Ruin a plank*
Hilary Brown	*I horny brawl*
Mister John Webber	*New jet bombs hirer!*
Betty Allen	*A belly tent*
Jennifer Paterson	*Na! Fine porn jester*
Clarissa Dickson Wright	*Darn! This girl sick as cow!*
Ross Burden	*Ruder snobs*
Sophie Grigson	*Gosh! Senior pig!*
Linda McCartney	*Mend carnal city*
Jane Grigson	*Join naggers*
The Naked Chef	*He deck fat hen*

COMPUTER GAMES AND CHARACTERS

Tomb Raider	*Drat! I'm bore*
Lara Croft	*Oral craft*
Resident Evil	*Devil entries*
Street Fighter	*Regret the fist*
Metal Gear Solid	*Dismal alter-ego*
The Mines of Moria	*I roam finest home*
Final Fantasy Seven	*Na! Envy fine fat lass*
Star Wars Racer	*Crass rear wart*
Ridge Racer Revolution	*Devour geriatric loner*
Total Carnage	*A cattle groan*
Lethal Enforcers	*Hello screen fart!*
Pinball Dreams	*Plasma blinder*
Sonic The Hedgehog	*Shhh! Entice God ego*
Super Mario Brothers	*I'm horror pest abuser*
Young Merlin	*Ugly iron men*
Football Manager	*Aloof bat-mangler*
Wing Commander	*Crown mega-mind*
Knightmare	*I thank germ*
Sensible Soccer	*Boss screen lice*
Duke Nukem Three	*Bless nice score*
Micropose Formula One	*Romp lunacies of Romeo*
Another World	*Wonder harlot*
Mario The Plumber	*A premium brothel*
Donkey Kong Country	*OK young trendy conk*
Superstar Ice Hockey	*Cheerio, pasty sucker!*

FAMOUS DISC JOCKEYS

Christopher Evans	*He's a rich TV person*
Jamie Theakston	*I'm the joke Satan*
Danny Baker	*Ran by, naked*
Tony Blackburn	*Blunt racy knob*
Jimmy Saville	*Evil slimy jam*
Mister John Peel	*Honest limp jeer*
Kenny Everett	*Key rent event*
Alan Freeman	*Earn male fan*
Pete Murray	*Mature prey*
Jimmy Young	*Yummy jingo*
Miranda Ward	*Inward drama*
Terry Wogan	*New rat orgy*
Simon Dee	*On demise*
Chris Tarrant	*Sir chart-rant*
Johnnie Walker	*Jerk while anon.*
Roger Day	*Ogre yard*
Ed Stewart	*Weed tarts*
Zoe Ball	*Oz label*
Bruno Brookes	*Bonus or broke*
David 'Kid' Jensen	*Jaded kind veins*
Mr Mike Smith	*Hmm! Miser kit*
Pat Sharpe	*Paper hats*
Jayne Middlemiss	*I'd jammy idleness*
Melanie Sykes	*Slime Yankees*
Nicky Campbell	*Calmly peck nib*

FASHION DESIGNERS

Laura Ashley	*Ha! USA, really.*
Saint Laurent	*Neutral stain*
Calvin Klein	*In naval lick*
Jean Paul Gaultier	*Alien jugular tape*
Yves St Laurent	*Lusty veterans*
Hubert de Givenchy	*The hungry vice bed*
Caroline Charles	*Real nice scholar*
Guy Laroche	*Oh! Cruel gay*
Pierre Cardin	*Randier price*
Christian Dior	*Is horrid antic*
Hattie Carnegie	*Eating a heretic*
Levi Strauss	*Ass rivulets*
Irene Galitzene	*Elite inner gaze*
Gabrielle Chanel	*A lechering label*
Giorgio Armani	*A! I grooming air*
Christian Lacroix	*I rich toxin rascal*
Ralph Lauren	*Hall rape! Run!*
Gianni Versace	*Naive creasing*
Miss Mary Quant	*A! My man's squirt*
Bruce Oldfield	*Fierce odd bull*
Scott Croala	*Lost car coat*
Zandra Rhodes	*Darn doze rash*
Catherine Walker	*Alien wreck-hater*
Jasper Conran	*Porn car jeans*
Betty Jackson	*Jacket by snot*

FEMALE SEX SYMBOLS

Melinda Messenger	*Me sneering damsel*
Natalie Imbruglia	*Rub me, I italian gal*
Yasmine Bleeth	*This able enemy*
Salma Hayek	*A shaky male*
Melanie Bratt	*Banal termite*
Chloe Annett	*The tan clone*
Caroline Corr	*Colon carrier*
Ulrika Jonsson	*No! Kiss journal*
Elizabeth Shue	*Huh! Bite sleaze*
Claire Richards	*Richer radicals*
Miss Samantha Janus	*Smash main ass junta*
Emma Noble	*Melon beam*
Miss Joanne Guest	*Jesus! Snot enigma*
Tiffani Amber Thiessen	*Feminine breasts faith*
Phillipa Forrester	*Hello! Fart is ripper*
Nicole Appleton	*Alien ponce plot*
Denise Richards	*Reddish arsenic*
Carmen Electra	*Rectal menacer*
Miss Donna Air	*In dross mania*
Cat Deeley	*Tele decay*
Claire Goose	*Calories ego*
Miss Kelly Brook	*My OK killer boss*
Sarah Michelle Gellar	*Illegal harsher camel*
Cameron Diaz	*Nazi comrade*
Andrea Corr	*Rear Conrad*

HOLLYWOOD LEADING MEN

Fred Astaire	*I feared rats*
James Stewart	*A warmest jest*
Humphrey Bogart	*Harm puberty hog*
Cary Grant	*Rat nag cry*
Marlon Brando	*Bald moron ran*
Henry Fonda	*One-hand fry*
Clark Gable	*Black lager*
James Cagney	*Gay scene jam*
Spencer Tracy	*A screen crypt*
Charlie Chaplin	*Pinch leach liar*
Gary Cooper	*Yo! Carp ogre*
Gregory Peck	*Grey cork peg*
Mister John Wayne	*Now in her majesty*
Laurence Oliver	*A violence ruler*
Gene Kelly	*Leg keenly*
Warren Beatty	*Watery banter*
Kirk Douglas	*US Kodak girl*
James Dean	*Jeans dame*
Burt Lancaster	*Blunt rear acts*
Eddie Murphy	*I'm hyped rude*
Buster Keaton	*Broken statue*
Sidney Poitier	*Is tidy pioneer*
Robert Mitchum	*I'm hotter crumb*
Edward G Robinson	*Weird dragon snob*
Steve McQueen	*Me TV sequence*

HOLLYWOOD LEADING WOMEN

Marlene Dietrich	*Nice Hitler dream*
Marilyn Monroe	*I marry loon men*
Elizabeth Taylor	*I the lazy bloater*
Mae West	*Am sweet*
Miss Joan Crawford	*Major's acid frowns*
Katherine Hepburn	*Eh! Herein bankrupt*
Bette Davis	*Betted visa*
Audrey Hepburn	*Her unready pub*
Ingrid Bergman	*Branding grime*
Greta Garbo	*Garbage rot*
Judy Garland	*Lady dung jar*
Barbara Stanwyck	*A raw crabby stank*
Claudette Colbert	*Collect brute date*
Grace Kelly	*Racy leg elk*
Ginger Rogers	*Regorge rings*
Vivien Leigh	*Evil gin hive*
Barbra Streisand	*Bad star is barren*
Shirley Temple	*The slimy leper*
Rita Hayworth	*Hot hairy wart*
Lauren Bacall	*A nuclear ball*
Sophia Loren	*One posh liar*
Miss Jean Harlow	*Jams heroin laws*
Carole Lombard	*More local drab*
Mary Pickford	*Form prick day*
Ava Gardner	*Veranda rag*

INFAMOUS CRIMINALS

Lee Harvey Oswald	*Who slay? Revealed!*
Herman Mudgett	*Madmen get hurt*
Albert DeSalvo	*Blasted a lover*
Ted Bundy	*Bend duty*
Jack The Ripper	*Cheap jerk trip*
Peter Sutcliffe	*It's perfect fuel*
David Berkowitz	*I bed TV wizard, OK?*
George Hennard	*Gangrened hero*
Bruno Richard Hauptmann	*Hurrah! Input drab conman*
Reggie Kray	*A key rigger*
Jeffrey Dahmer	*Her jam fry feed*
Charles Manson	*Charmless anon*
Myra Hindley	*Laid my Henry*
Ian Brady	*In bra day*
William Joyce	*Limey jail cow*
Sir Roger Casement	*I'm secret groaners*
Patty Hearst	*Ha! Tarty pest*
Peter Kurtin	*Erupt tinker*
Daniel M'Naghten	*I'm hand entangle*
Orenthal James Simpson	*Simpleton hen ass major*
John Christie	*Shh! I injector*
Douglas Daniel Clark	*A odd slug like carnal*
Ed Gein	*Gene ID*
John Wayne Gacy	*Na! Gay wench joy*
Albert Fish	*I flesh brat*

MALE SEX SYMBOLS

Stephen Gately	*The elegant spy*
Pierce Brosnan	*Is barren ponce*
Luke Goss	*Egos sulk*
Danny Wahlberg	*Held brawny nag*
Popstar Ricky Martin	*Cranky traitor pimps*
Mister Brad Pitt	*Best armpit dirt*
Timothy Dalton	*Oh my! Not lad tit*
Colin Firth	*Thin frolic*
Paul Danan	*Animal pad*
Mister Tom Jones	*Moron's jest time*
Julio Inglesias	*Is alien soil jug*
Charles Bronson	*He snarls bronco*
Bob Mortimer	*Boob trimmer*
Brendan Fraser	*Render fan's bra*
Henry Rollins	*Sorry hell inn*
Jerome Flynn	*Mr. Fennel Joy*
Robson Greene	*Born ego sneer*
Actor Nick Berry	*Born tacky crier*
Barry White	*Weary birth*
Emilio Estevez	*Seize love item*
Billy Warlock	*Lack willy orb*
Steven Segal	*Get NES slave*
Rob Lowe	*Loo brew*
Tom Selleck	*OK smell etc*
Mr. Joseph Fiennes	*Joins hempen serf*

MODELS

Karen Mulder	*Me real drunk*
Tyra Banks	*Yank's brat*
Melissa Tkautz	*Kit amazes slut*
Heidi Klum	*Helium kid*
Laetibitia Casta	*I abet attic alias*
Gabi Simson	*I am bog sins*
Lisa Snowdon	*I down salons*
Cindy Crawford	*Fry candid crow*
Kate Moss	*Met OK ass*
Elle Macphearson	*Hall poser menace*
Natasha Henstridge	*Na! The randiest shag*
Claudia Schiffer	*Fear acidic flush*
Sophie Anderton	*I ensnared photo*
Katie Richmond	*Thicker domain*
Model Nell McAndrew	*Mend colder man well*
Caprice	*Race pic*
Helena Christensen	*Ensnares thin leech*
Naomi Campbell	*Manic beam poll*
Sarah Parish	*Has rash pair*
Debby Carr	*Dreary BBC*
Christie Turlington	*The instruction girl*
Linda Evangelista	*Na! A Devil's genital*
Linda Lusardi	*Laid lads' ruin*
Model Jerry Hall	*Arm jelly holder*
Rhona Mitra	*Harm ration*

NOBEL PRIZE WINNERS

Samuel Ting	*Ugliest man*
Martin Luther King	*Ugh! Tart in Kremlin*
David Trimble	*Dim devil brat*
John Hume MEP	*Oh! He jump men*
Jane Addams	*Jaded as man*
Pearl S. Buck	*Pub slacker*
Ralph Bunche	*Herbal punch*
'Papa' Hemmingway	*Ahem! Wimpy pagan*
Albert A. Michelson	*Lamebrain clothes*
Woodrow Wilson	*Sworn loo widow*
Mister Sinclair Lewis	*In silliest war-crimes*
Eugene O'Neill	*Glue on Eileen*
William Faulkner	*Kill weariful man*
George Marshall	*Gosh! Larger male*
John Steinback	*Ha! Inject knobs*
Henry Kissinger	*Sink heresy grin*
Le Duc Tho	*The cloud*
Saul Bellow	*Soluble law*
Milton Friedman	*Main demon flirt*
Mister William Lipscomb Jr	*Mimic worst sperm jail bill*
Baruch Blumberg	*Blubber chum rag*
Daniel Carleton Gajdusek	*Acute slandering lad joke*
Burton Richter	*Burnt Rhetoric*
Mairead Corrigan	*I am a dragon crier*
Betty Williams	*Blast limey wit!*

PHOTOGRAPHERS

Leslie Krims	*Is mere skill*
Ernst Haas	*Sane trash*
Serge Lutens	*Lens gesture*
Duane Michals	*Child nauseam*
Bernard Plossu	*Lab rubs person*
Linda Benedict Jones	*Inject bonded aliens*
Norman Parkinson	*O man! In porn ranks*
Roman Cieslewicz	*Comical wren size*
Lennart Nilsson	*Linen snot snarl*
Ralph Morse	*Lash romper*
Robert Capa	*Bare rat cop*
William Eugene Smith	*Eliminate while smug*
Robert Demachy	*Botchy dreamer*
Susan Meiselas	*Slain masseuse*
Arnold Newman	*Landowner man*
Analoli Garanin	*Rain on all again*
Cecil Beaton	*Celibate con*
Sam Haskins	*Has man kiss*
David Bailey	*Ya! I bad devil*
Lucien Clergue	*Urge uncle lice*
Charles Harbutt	*Shh! Curable tart*
Ralph Gibson	*Harping slob*
Josef Sudek	*Fussed joke*
David Seidner	*Divine dreads*
Robert Doisneau	*A riotous bender*

ROYALTY

Princess Diana	*Ascend in Paris*
Sarah Ferguson	*Na! Shag for sure!*
His Royal Highness The Prince Of Wales	*Sly, harsh English poser, I cheat on wife*
Princess Anne	*Nice spanners*
William Windsor	*Swim in wild oral*
Prince Edward	*Weird carp den*
Princess Margaret	*Grr! Satanism creep*
Andrew Windsor	*Warned in words*
Prince Phillip	*Rich lip nipple*
Mary Queen Of Scots	*My conquest of arse*
Elizabeth Tudor	*Hi! Blue doze tart*
Mary Tudor	*Rotary mud*
Queen Victoria	*Quite vain core*
Princess Beatrice	*Inter-species crab*
Princess Eugenie	*Insecure seeping*
King Edward	*New drag kid*
The Queen Mother	*Met hot queer hen*
Prince Harry	*Rear inch pry*
King Henry The Eighth	*Hey! The night gherkin*
Queen Elizabeth	*The equine blaze*
King Charles The Second	*He's the slandering cock*
King Richard The Second	*Stronger inch dickhead*
King James The Second	*Smashing decent joke*
King Edward The Sixth	*X-rated wish knighted*
Princess Stephanie Of Monaco	*She is a fine non-compact poser*

SCIENTISTS & INVENTORS

Dmitri Ivanovich Mendeleyev	*Ahem! It involved divine mercy*
Albert Einstein	*Ten elite brains*
Charles Augustin de Coulomb	*Behold genius's accumulator*
Marie Curie	*I rue crimea*
Edward Goodrich Acheson	*Oh god! New hard-core acids*
Isaac Newton	*Nice as a town*
Henry Cavendish	*Envy hard inches*
Jules Henri Poincare	*Join raunchier sleep*
Orville Wright	*Throw evil girl*
Werner Heisenberg	*Her beginner sewer*
Michael Faraday	*A mad fairy leach*
James Prescott Joule	*Oops! Just male reject*
Robert Fludd	*Bed turf lord*
Sir James Dewar	*Raid jaw sewers*
Robert Boyle	*'Rebel boy' rot*
Nicholas Sadi Carnot	*Anarchic sadist loon*
Thomas Young	*Oh no! Gay smut*
Pierre Curie	*Rue ripe crier*
Andre Marie Ampere	*Me drearier apeman*
Alessandro Volta	*Love-lorn ass data*
Georges Leclanche	*Clenches large ego*
Georg Simon Ohm	*Homo groin gems*
James Clerk Maxwell	*Smell wax camel jerk*
Sir Joseph John Thomson	*Shh! Join jest-shop moron*
Alexander Fleming	*Na! Flexed malinger*

SPY FILMS

The Scarlet Pimpernel	*Three mental cripples*
Mata Hari	*Ha! I'm a rat*
Night Train To Munich	*Rotting inhuman itch*
Golden Earrings	*Slandering ogre*
The Spy In Black	*Key bitch plans*
Five Graves To Cairo	*Vicar's favourite ego*
Cloak And Dagger	*Lacked gonad rage*
The Man Who Never Was	*Heavens! Women wrath*
The Counterfeit Traitor	*Truth if rotate erection*
The Lady Vanishes	*Hate shady snivel*
Across The Pacific	*Carp ethics fiasco*
Foreign Correspondent	*Sod referencing to porn*
Three Days of the Condor	*Ho ho! Defy censored tart*
The Deadly Affair	*Fiery fathead lad*
Watch on the Rhine	*Enchant with hero*
The Iron Curtain	*Incinerator hut*
The Spy Who Came In From The Cold	*Sweet Mary! I month-old chop chef*
Ministry Fear	*In fart misery*
The Quiller Memorandum	*I'm not queer dull hammer!*
The Parallax View	*Raw laxative help*
Escape To Nowhere	*Now echoes repeat*
Executive Action	*Excite nova cutie*
The Great Manhunt	*The hung mean tart*
Walk East On Beacon	*Weak blast on ocean*
Decision Before Dawn	*Base confined weirdo*

AMERICAN & AFRICAN COUNTRIES

Dominica	*I'm on Acid*
Surinam	*Am ruins*
Republic Of Uruguay	*You peculiar furbug*
Venezuela	*Laze venue*
United States of America	*Mafia tease destruction*
Antigua And Barbuda	*Rutabage band and I*
Republic Of Algeria	*Facile pig labourer*
Republic Of Angola	*A fine globular cop*
Republic of Argentina	*Bloating unfair creep*
Central African Republic	*Fine circular crab planet*
Burkina Faso	*Sink Arab UFO*
Kingdom Of Lesotho	*I'm hooked flog snot*
Ivory Coast	*Sooty vicar*
Republic of Guatemala	*Blame graceful utopia*
Eritrea	*Rare tie*
Equatorial Guinea	*Agile quota in urea*
Republic of Mauritania	*Pure Mafia lubrication*
United Mexican States	*Sex-mad acne institute*
Kingdom Of Morocco	*Good if common rock*
Mozambique	*Me quiz a mob*
Kingdom Of Swaziland	*Now I'm dazing flak sod*
Republic Of Congo	*Clip bouncer goof*
Republic Of Zimbabwe	*Blew up fabric zombie*
Republic Of Tanzania	*Unzip raincoat fable*
Sierra Leone	*Release iron*

AMERICAN TOURIST ATTRACTIONS

Mount Shasta	*Satan's mouth*
Arlington National Cemetery	*Ignorant teeny American toll*
Sear's Tower	*Worse rates*
Disneyland	*Lady sinned*
The Washington Memorial	*Memo annihilates growth*
Hollywood Boulevard	*Bury lewd voodoo hall*
Universal Studios	*Industrious slave*
US Space And Rocket Center	*Sucker corpse attendance*
Kenai Peninsula	*Nuke asinine pal*
Montezuma Castle	*Close mutant maze*
Organ Pipe National Monument	*Rampant unemotional opening*
The World Of Coca-Cola	*Chocolate crowd loaf*
Big Bend National Park	*Abandoning bleak trip*
Mount Rushmore	*Mourn hero smut*
Wind Cave, Dakota	*A wink advocated*
Devil's Tower, Dakota	*Rowdiest vodka tale*
Disney World	*Old dry swine*
Kennedy Space Center	*Sentenced creep yank*
Plymouth Rock	*Holy muck port*
Everglades National Park	*Save dragon-like prenatal*
Florida Keys	*O! Frail dykes*
The Grand Canyon	*Not randy change*
Indianapolis Motor Speedway	*Na! Sloppy wearisome addition*
Library Of Congress	*Nearby gross frolic*
The Lincoln Memorial	*Manomentric lino hell*

AMERICAN TOWNS & CITIES

Burkittsville, Maryland	*Evil kills my drab truant*
Kansas City	*Satanic sky*
Salt Lake City	*Tackily stale*
Boston, MA	*Nob atoms*
Cape Cod, MA	*Mad ace cop*
Philadelphia	*Ha! Idle hip pal*
Washington DC	*Hang disc town*
New York City	*Yo! Tiny wreck*
New Orleans	*Loner wanes*
Pittsburgh	*Tight burps*
Indianapolis	*A sin pain idol*
Detroit	*Diet rot*
Minneapolis	*I'm Lenin's OAP*
Tampa Bay, Florida	*Tap mafia broadly*
Milwaukee	*I weak mule*
Dallas, Texas	*Sex lad atlas*
Las Vegas	*Gas slave*
Houston, Texas	*Shoot sex aunt*
Los Angeles	*Legal noses*
San Diego	*Agonised*
Seattle	*Test ale*
Anchorage	*Organ ache*
Denver, Colorado	*Reveal odd croon*
San Antonio	*No, No! I Satan*
Chicago, Illinois	*Hi! A silicon logic*

BRITISH TOURIST ATTRACTIONS

Houses Of Parliament	*Loonies far up Thames*
Jane Austen's House	*The nauseous Jane's*
Regent's Park	*Regret spank*
Royal Academy Of Arts	*Drama acolyte's foray*
Natural History Museum	*Ultra-mysterious human*
The Temple Church	*Clutch hemp there*
Woburn Abbey	*Now bury babe*
St George's Chapel	*Preaches toggles*
Legoland, Windsor	*Wild Londoner gas*
Windsor Great Park	*Poker art drawings*
SS Great Britain	*Rabies starting*
Duxfords Airfield	*Did fix fraud loser*
Stonehenge	*Get no sheen*
The British Museum	*Emeritus thumbs 'hi'.*
Buckingham Palace	*UK Cable Campaign*
Cabinet War Rooms	*Worst maniac bore*
Peak District	*Is picked tart*
Imperial War Museum	*I'm a sure wimp mauler*
Thomas Hardy's Cottage	*Oh my! Castrated a ghost*
London Planetarium	*Polaroid annulment*
Madame Tussauds	*Sad data museums*
National Portrait Gallery	*Inane tarty gorilla patrol*
The Lake District	*The idle sick tart*
Lands End, Cornwall	*Slander clown land*
National Railway Musuem	*I'm womanly nausea ritual*

CAPITAL CITIES

Vienna, Austria	*Invites an aura*
London, England	*Golden land? 'Non!'*
Sofia, Bulgaria	*I grab foul Asia*
Ottowa City, Canada	*A two-day catatonic*
Bejing City, China	*Cynic hating jibe*
Santiago, Chile	*Isolating ache*
San Jose, Costa Rica	*As actors join case*
Brussels, Belgium	*Bless glum bruise*
Canberra, Australia	*A cranial rat abuser*
Rangoon, Burma	*O man! Organ rub*
Paris, France	*A finer scrap*
Bang Kok, Thailand	*Had a talking knob*
Taipei, Taiwan	*I await ant pie*
Jerusalem, Israel	*Real Jesus mailer*
Stockholm, Sweden	*Slow demon sketch*
Madrid, Spain	*Is damp drain*
Seoul, South Korea	*Eureka! Loo shouts*
Dublin, Ireland	*Blinded urinal*
Moscow, Russia	*I'm sour cow ass*
Manila, Phillipines	*Pal in nihilism leap*
Lisbon, Portugal	*In globular spot*
Bucharest, Romania	*I am a trash bouncer*
Panama City	*A! A tiny camp*
Islamabad, Pakistan	*Blast! I am a spank aid*
Wellington, New Zealand	*A new golden Lenin waltz*

ENGLISH TOWNS & CITIES

Cambridge	*Bred magic*
Newcastle-under-Lyme	*Drew lunacy elements*
Manchester	*Tense charm*
Southend-On-Sea	*Ha! Nudeness too*
Basingstoke, Hants	*Thanking asbestos*
Blackpool, Lancashire	*Lacks parochial noble*
Chichester	*This creche*
Sheffield, England	*Dangled fine flesh*
Princetown	*Twerp in con*
Birmingham City	*Any bright mimic*
Cheltenham	*Lech anthem*
Stratford-Upon-Avon	*Not vast porno fraud*
Northampton	*Torn phantom*
Stoke-On-Trent	*Rotten tokens*
Peterborough	*Huge rot probe*
Berwick-Upon-Tweed	*Wipe wonder bucket*
Newcastle	*Acne welts*
Grassington	*Storing nags*
Liverpool, England	*Long evildoer plan*
Cockermouth	*Hot muck core*
Carlisle	*Ill races*
Worcester	*Erect rows*
Henley-On-Thames	*Opens healthy menu*
Okehampton	*Na! Kept homo*
Buckfastleigh	*Huge black fits*

EUROPEAN & ASIAN COUNTRIES

Liechtenstein	*Lenient ethics*
Afghanistan	*Has giant fan*
Great Britain	*Arbitrate gin*
State Of Israel	*Earliest fatso*
Republic Of Albania	*Incapable of burial*
Principality Of Andorra	*Paranoid flop irritancy*
Swiss Confederation	*So fine randiest cows*
Belgium	*Big mule*
Belorussia	*Soil abuser*
Kingdom Of Bhutan	*God! Monk fun habit*
Bosnia - Herzegovina	*Oh no! seize bargain*
Sultanate Of Brunei	*Tut if unreasonable*
Bulgaria	*A bug lair*
Kingdom Of Cambodia	*I am mocking bad food*
Kingdom Of Denmark	*God! Freak mind monk*
Republic Of China	*Chop if incurable*
Russian Federation	*A fine rude arsonist*
Republic of Germany	*Becoming prayerful*
Republic Of Iraq	*Bare frolic quip*
Republic Of Ireland	*Clarified blue porn*
State Of Kuwait	*Saw it fake tout*
Principality Of Monaco	*Fornication policy map*
Kingdom Of Nepal	*Mad plonking foe*
Kingdom Of Norway	*I'm darn wonky goof*
Republic Of Poland	*A foul crippled nob*

EUROPEAN TOWNS & CITIES

Vatican City	*I vacant city*
Dusseldorf	*Furled sods*
Bucharest	*Brute cash*
Archangel	*Gnarl ache*
Copenhagen	*Hog penance*
Bratislava	*Saliva brat*
Strasbourg	*Robust rags*
Trondheim	*Dim throne*
St Petersburg	*Best pert rugs*
Stuttgart, Germany	*Smutty nagger tart*
Florence, Italy	*Entirely focal*
Toulouse	*O! Sue lout*
Volgograd, Russia	*Ga-ga drools virus*
Salonica, Greece	*Agencies' oracle*
Stavanger	*Ant Graves*
Maastricht	*Static harm*
Eindhoven, Netherlands	*Enthrone sniveled hand*
The Hague	*Huge hate*
Marseille	*Real slime*
Athens, Greece	*Cheater genes*
Salamanca	*As almanac*
Palermo	*Ale romp*
Innsbruck	*Brick nuns*
Katowice	*Coke wait*
Warsaw, Poland	*Load war spawn*

GLOBAL TOURIST ATTRACTIONS

The Louvre	*True hovel*
Ayers Rock	*Rocky arse*
The Great Wall Of China	*Altogether, chain flaw*
Sydney Opera House	*Up on shady eyesore*
The Kremlin	*Tinker helm*
The Spanish Riding School	*Hating poor childishness*
The Great Barrier Reef	*Tiger fart bearer here*
Musee Des Beaux Arts	*Abused extrema sues*
Red Square, Moscow	*Am queer cow dross*
Tiananmen Square	*Meen quarantines*
The Eiffel Tower	*Feel hotter wife*
Bird Market	*Embark dirt*
Alice Springs	*Special grins*
The Acropolis	*Copies harlot*
Connemara National Park	*Ancient paranormal koan*
Brera Palace	*Capable rear*
St Basil's Cathedral	*This blasted rascal*
St Mark's Square, Venice	*Caveman squirts asker*
The Roman Forum	*Form hot manure*
The Sistine Chapel	*Shines telepathic*
The Forbidden City	*Tired botchy fiend*
The Parthenon	*Then hate porn*
Temple Of Athena Nike	*Female kite pantheon*
Mao's Mausoleum	*Some usual ammo*
The Little Mermaid, Denmark	*Met idle Kremlin mad hatter*

HISTORIC BRITISH CASTLES

Alnwick Castle	*Lack incest law*
Blair Castle	*Racist label*
Broughton Castle	*Once brutal ghost*
Caernarvon Castle	*Satan cancer lover*
Castle Ashby	*Beastly cash*
Castlecoole, Northern Ireland	*Nice rotten alcohol slanderer*
Castle Howard	*Claret shadow*
Chirk Castle	*Cricket lash*
Crathes Castle	*Cattle chasers*
Dunster Castle	*Classed nutter*
Glamis Castle	*Slag climates*
Inveraray Castle	*Secretarial navy*
Lullingstone Castle	*Counselling tallest*
Penrhyn Castle	*Lynches parent*
Powis Castle	*Cowpat's isle*
Rockingham Castle	*The alarming cocks*
Sizergh Castle	*Glazier chests*
Sudeley Castle	*Lately seduces*
Tamworth Castle	*Threw total scam*
Warwick Castle	*Is wet crack law*
Highclere Castle	*Heretic shag cell*
Windsor Castle	*Clown disaster*
Kimbolton Castle	*Bitten small cook*
St Mawes Castle	*Wet classmates*
Appleby Castle	*Play cable pest*

HISTORIC BRITISH GARDENS

Swiss Garden	*Grew sad sins*
The Savill Garden	*Dangle evil trash*
Stowe Landscape Gardens	*Enlarged cowpat sadness*
Bodnant Gardens	*Darn bent gonads*
Hidcote Manor Gardens	*Hard-core demon giants*
Nymans Garden	*Randy men nags*
Acorn Bank Garden	*Darn knob carnage*
Hardstoft Herb Gardens	*Short grandfather beds*
Compton Acres Gardens	*Massaged porn concert*
Hodges Barn Gardens	*Darned gnasher's bog*
Exbury Gardens	*Sex drug nearby*
Houghton Lodge Gardens	*Hold the gangrenous dog*
Burford House Gardens	*Beg horrendous frauds*
Spetchley Park Garden	*Help! Strange dyke crap*
The Gardens Of The Rose	*For greenest hotheads*
Great Comp Gardens	*Compared gangster*
Mount Ephraim Gardens	*Rampaged nourishment*
Owl House Gardens	*Now huge sad loser*
Royal Botanic Gardens	*Ascending laboratory*
Hoveton Hall Gardens	*Oh hell! Gonad servant*
Coton Manor Garden	*Arrogant demon con*
Haddonstone Show Garden	*Now darned hothead snogs*
Holdenby House Gardens	*Shy loser dung bonehead*
Botanic Gardens, Belfast	*Bloating bastard's fence*
Harlow Carr Botanical Gardens	*Anarchic arrogant lad bowlers*

LAKES

Lake Athabasca	*Aha! Black as tea*
Lake Malawi	*I'm all awake*
Lake Michigan	*I'm a leach king*
Lake Superior	*Perilous rake*
Lake Victoria	*A trivial coke*
Lake Huron	*A hunk role*
Lake Tanganyika	*Leaky tank again*
Great Bear Lake	*Large tea-break*
Lake Baykal	*A leaky balk*
Great Slave Lake	*Skeletal ravage*
Lake Windermere	*I am a keener lewd*
Lake Winnipeg	*Wipe angel ink*
Lake Ontario	*Oriental oak*
Lake Ladoga	*OK, a glad ale*
Lough Neagh	*Hug halogen*
Lough Derg	*Oh! Gurgled*
Loch Lomond, Ireland	*Man! Old children loo*
Lake Prespa	*Papal reeks*
The Balaton Lake	*A bleak ant hotel*
The Great Salt Lake	*Skeletal earth tag*
Lake Alaotra	*A koala alert*
Lake George	*O! Large geek*
Mcleod Lake	*Me cold lake*
Lake Manitoba	*Main boat leak*
Williston Lake	*Let's walk in oil*

MOUNTAINS

The Alps	*He splat!*
The Ural Mountains	*Isn't autumnal hero*
The Mourne Mountains	*Ho! Monument urinates*
The Black Mountain	*This ambulance knot*
Wicklow Mountains	*Miscount wino walk*
The Cumbrian Mountains	*I'm not a subhuman cretin*
Ben Lomond	*Old nob men*
Ben Cruachan	*Urban chance*
Mountains of Antrim	*I'm not Satan uniform!*
Mullaghmore Mountains	*Loathing normal museum*
Errigal Mountain	*Tailoring manure*
Blue Stack Mountains	*Not sustainable muck*
Slieve Bloom Mountains	*Entomb some villainous*
Knockmealdown Mountains	*Now madmen skunk location*
Derrynasaggart Mountains	*Smartarse orangutan dying*
Mount Everest	*Utmost veneer*
Snowy Mountains	*Anonymous twins*
Mount Wilhelm	*Well in hot mum*
Mount Elbert	*Molten brute*
Stikine Mountains	*Nukes intimations*
Mackensie Mountains	*Muckiest insane moan*
Caribou Mountains	*I'm a innocuous brat*
Rocky Mountains	*Yank consortium*
Bighorn Mountains	*Is not boring human*
Sacramento Mountians	*Neat monstrous maniac*

RIVERS

The River Thames	*Have mere thirst*
The River Shannon	*In her snort haven*
The Eden River	*Reverent hide*
The River Clyde	*Divert lechery*
The River Lagan	*Rat girl heaven*
The Liffey	*Filthy fee*
The Blackwater River	*Evil brat wreck earth*
The River Bann	*Invent her bra*
The River Moy	*My! I've her rot*
The Guadalquivir River	*Hirer gave virtual quid*
The Loire River	*Her evil rioter*
The Pescara River	*Archive rear pest*
The Vindel River	*Invert evil herd*
The Manych River	*Never a rich myth*
The Mississippi River	*Primitives' ship rises*
The Songhua Jiang River	*He just ravaging heroin*
The Godavari River	*A rather vivid gore*
The Darling River	*Grr! The evil drain*
The River Sabine	*Severe brain hit*
The River Nile	*Her inert evil*
The Amazon River	*Hi! Remove Tarzan*
The Tanaro River	*Hotter vain rear*
The River Mackensie	*Ahem! Stink receiver*
The Volga River	*A grovel thrive*
The Amur	*Hate rum*

SCOTTISH TOWNS & CITIES

Dumfries	*Mud fires*
Stranraer	*Rarer tans*
Cairnryan	*Cry Narnia*
Caithness	*Ethnic ass*
Paisley	*I spy ale*
Stirling	*Girl's nit*
Perthshire	*He strip her*
Strathearn	*Ha! Rent star*
Aberdeen	*A beer den*
Coldstream	*Mold traces*
Berwick-upon-Tweed	*We burn wicked poet*
Galashiels	*Shag allies*
Selkirk Town	*Tinkle works*
Greenock	*Ogre neck*
Blantyre, Scotland	*Clean tarty blonds*
Galloway	*Loyal wag*
Kirkcudbright	*Kick birth drug*
Newton Stewart	*We two entrants*
Wigtown, Scotland	*It clags downtown*
Inveraray	*Rainy rave*
Portpatrick	*Rat prick pot*
Aviemore	*I mere ova*
Arbroath	*Ha! Rot bra*
Kinross Town	*No! Stink rows*
Kilmartin Glen	*A Kremlin glint*

SEAS & OCEANS

The Irish Sea	*He raise this*
The English Channel	*Enhancing the hells*
The Black Sea	*Bleak cheats*
The Dead Sea	*Sedate head*
The Pacific Ocean	*A chief acne topic*
The North Atlantic Ocean	*Continental throat ache*
The Indian Ocean	*No! The inane acid*
The South Atlantic Ocean	*Ouch! On the tactile Satan*
The Southern Ocean	*Ho ho! Enter nutcase*
The Coral Sea	*Last ace hero*
The Tasman Sea	*Satan hates me*
Ross Sea	*Sore ass*
Mozambique Channel	*Melanoma bench quiz*
The Weddell Sea	*Seeded wealth*
The Arctic Ocean	*Choice reactant*
The Barents Sea	*Senate bathers*
North Sea	*Trash one*
South China Sea	*Tenacious hash*
The Sea Of Okhotsk	*Hot fat seeks hook*
The Red Sea	*Hate reeds*
The Caspian Sea	*A satanic sheep!*
The Mediterranean Sea	*Harm earnest detainee*
The Baltic Sea	*Ethical beast*
The Arafura Sea	*Shut a fear area*
The Yellow Sea	*Hey! Lowest ale*

UNIVERSITIES & COLLEGES

University College, London	*Gloriously invented clone*
University Of East Anglia	*Setisfying re-evaluation*
University Of Buckingham	*Furious envy-making bitch*
University Of Edinburgh	*Furthering divine buoys*
Queen's University	*Is urine envy quest*
Harvard University	*Ravish randy virtue*
Oxford University	*Sod fury vixen riot*
Cambridge University	*Is grim deviancy brute*
University Of Wales	*Weary sinful soviet*
University Of Birmingham	*I'm the boring virus infamy*
Brunel University	*Virile sunny brute*
Croydon College	*Once coldly ogre*
Cranfield University	*Rancidly fine virtues*
Yale University	*Evil unity years*
University Of Luton	*Nutty foul revision*
Leeds College Of Music	*Melodic Colleges fuse*
University Of Glasgow	*Now glossary fugitive*
University Of East London	*No! Devoutly fine arsonist*
De Montfort University	*Notify tormented virus*
Coventry University	*City survey inventor*
City University	*Icy entity virus*
University Of Aberdeen	*Fine dire suave rent-boy*
Kidderminster College	*Disliked erect mongrel*
University Of Hull	*Viler youthful sin*
University Of Essex	*Notifies sex survey*

AMERICAN POLITICIANS OF THE 1960S & 1970S

Edmund Muskie	*Nuked dummies*
Spiro Agnew	*Grow a penis*
Wayne Morse	*Some yawner*
Douglas Dillon	*Good dull snail*
Melvin Laird	*Ran mild evil*
Eugene McCarthy	*Ah! Emergency cut*
Albert Gore	*Rear goblet*
Everett Dirksen	*Reserved kitten*
Ross Barnett	*Snob starter*
George Wallace	*Eager legal cow*
Henry Kissinger	*Grey skin shrine*
Senator Frank Church	*Funk horn characters*
Barry Goldwater	*Large rowdy brat*
Hubert Humphrey	*He hurt hyper bum*
Robert Weaver	*Rear brew vote*
Edmund Brown	*Drowned numb*
Abraham Ribicoff	*Arch bimbo affair*
Robert McNamara	*Am brat romancer*
Senator Birch Bayh	*Shh! Arabic rent-boy*
George Romney	*O my! Green ogre*
Defense Secretary Clark Clifford	*Self-centred lad's iffy rock career*
Shirley Chisholm	*Shy heroism chill*
William Rogers	*I am slower girl*
Mister George McGovern	*Ever groggier comments*
James Rhodes	*Jeer sham sod*

AMERICAN POLITICIANS OF THE 1980S & 1990S

Ross Perot	*Pro tosser*
Michael Dukakis	*I am a kicked lush*
Stanislaw Kania	*Is a satin walk-in*
Edward Koch	*Whacked rod*
Warren Christopher	*Rich shower partner*
Mister Newt Gingrich	*Nice right wing monster*
Alexander M. Haig	*Aha! I Marx legend*
Harrison A. Williams	*A similar shown liar*
Harold Washington	*Now dashing harlot*
Carl Perkins	*Pricks learn*
Michael D. Barens	*Charmed lesbian*
Walter F. Mondale	*No well-made fart*
Geraldine Ferraro	*Ordering real fear*
Richard Lugar	*Arch drug liar*
Daniel Inouye	*Yo! I nude alien*
George Shultz	*Go chug seltzer*
Ted Kennedy	*Net dyke den*
Mister Dan Quayle	*Nastily mad queer*
Politician Jack Kemp	*Main pick-pocket jail*
Mr David Dinkins	*Mind drinks diva*
Madeleine Albright	*Giant dame here, Bill!*
George Pataki	*Karate pig ego*
Senator Bob Dole	*Bored beast loon*
Senator Jesse Helms	*Slosh jester enemas*
Pat Buchanan	*Ban a nut chap*

BRITISH POLITICIANS BEFORE 1960

Anthony Eden	*The nanny ode*
Neville Chamberlain	*In male vibrance hell*
Lloyd George	*Googly elder*
Clement Atlee PM	*Elect temple man*
Ernest Bevin	*Invents beer*
Herbert Morrison	*Tribesmen horror*
William Beveridge	*I believed grim law*
Kingsley Wood	*Godly swine OK*
A. Bonar Law	*An Arab low*
Leo Amery	*Mole year*
Lord Hitchingbrooke	*Horrid looking bench*
Ralph Assheton	*Hate slash porn*
Henry Willink	*Whinny killer*
R.A. Butler	*Brat rule*
Harold Laski	*Kills a hoard*
Aneurin Bevan	*A uneven brain*
Hugh Dalton	*Hog lad hunt*
Ellen Wilkinson	*Known ill senile*
Chuter Ede	*Thee crude*
George Tomlinson	*Ongoing molester*
Stafford Cripps	*Drops stiff carp*
Arthur Greenwood	*Huge reward on rot*
James Griffith	*Jam sheriff git*
Philip Noel Baxter	*Exploit brain help*
Mr David Maxwell Fyfe	*Fix mad lewd farm levy*

CONSERVATIVE POLITICIANS OF THE 1960S AND 1970S

Harold Macmillan	*Ill choral madman*
Margaret Hilda Thatcher	*Ha! The large rich mad tart!*
Peter Thorneycroft	*The creepy rot front*
Duncan Sandys	*Sad nuns candy*
Enoch Powell	*Hell! Open cow*
Nigel Birch	*I bench girl*
Derick Heathcoat Amory	*Okay! I'm the hardcore act*
Iain Macleod	*I demoniacal*
Reginald Maudling	*Alarming idle dung*
Tam Galbraith	*Grab that mail*
Quintin Hogg Hailsham	*Oh! I quit hash mangling*
Edward Heath	*Wet hard head*
Martin Redmayne	*Tiny dreamer man*
Edward Boyle	*Old weary bed*
Alec Douglas-Home	*Madhouse college*
Sir Keith Joseph	*Oi, shh!I jerk pets*
Mark Carlisle	*Lack slim rear*
Anthony Barber	*Hey! Brat 'n' baron*
Hugh Fraser	*Her fur hags*
Peter Walker	*Wet leper ark*
Geoffrey Rippon	*Rope porn effigy*
James Prior	*Oi! Sperm jar*
Michael Fraser	*A crime flasher*
Right Honorable John Nott, MP	*Jam on hot brothel porn night*
Rt. Hon. Airey Neave, MP	*Yeah! Pervert in moan*

CONSERVATIVE POLITICIANS OF THE 1980S & 1990S

Jonathan Aitken, perjury defendant	*Thief and a jerk and unrepentant - joy!*
William Hague	*Laugh? I wail, me*
Virginia Bottomley	*I'm an evil Tory bigot*
Norman Lamont	*Not normal man*
Michael Heseltine	*He is the ill menace*
Kenneth Clarke, MP	*Lent knacker hemp*
Harry Greenway, MP	*Hyper wary German*
Peter Lilley	*Reptile yell*
Nigel Lawson	*We all sign on*
Ex-Prime Minister John Major	*Jeer Marxism morphine joint*
Geoffrey Howe	*Hey! ogre of few*
Norman Tebbit	*No! I'm bent brat*
David Howell	*Had wild love*
David Mellor	*Am old drivel*
Leon Brittan	*Bitten 'n oral*
Nicholas Ridley	*Hardly silicone*
Michael Portillo	*Mr Political Hole*
Cecil Parkinson	*In prince's cloak*
Michael Howard	*Ahem! Wild roach*
Patrick Mayhew	*Ta! Wimpy hacker*
Edwina Currie	*Ice urine ward*
Brian Mawhinney	*Aha! I'm brew ninny*
Julian Critchley, MP	*The clinical jury*
Gillian Shephard	*Shh! Pleading liar*
Teresa Gorman	*O Man! Gets rear*

GOVERNMENT DEPARTMENTS

Agriculture	*Cruel guitar*
Cabinet Office	*A bionic effect*
Ministry Of Defence	*Sniffed my erection*
Education And Employment	*Dominant enemy copulated*
Environment	*Intern venom*
Foreign And Commonwealth Office	*Oh man! Coward on coffee-time fling*
Forestry Commission	*SOS! Rectify moronism*
Department of Health	*Often help mad hatter*
Customs And Excise	*Sex seduction scam*
The Home Office	*Chief homo feet*
Board Of Inland Revenue	*Devoured a infernal nob*
International Development	*Noted pertinent animal lover*
Lord Advocate's Department	*Detracts odd prenatal move*
Lord Chancellor's Department	*Cholesterol cramp trend land*
Northern Ireland Office	*Fine hard-core front-line*
Prime Minister's Office	*I'm fierce misfit person*
Privy Council Office	*Puffy civil coercion*
Scottish Office	*I chose tit scoff*
Social Security	*Saucy lice riots*
Trade And Industry	*Drat it! Randy nudes*
The Welsh Office	*Fetch lowish fee*
Crown Office For Scotland	*Stiff coward fool concern*
Scottish Courts Administration	*So dictators charm institutions*
Northern Ireland Court Service	*Enrich recursive Londoner tart*
Export Credits Guarantee	*Great X-rated persecution*

MEMBERS OF THE HOUSE OF LORDS

Desmond Ackner	*Cranked demons*
John Thomas Alderdice	*Join coldhearted sham*
David Alton	*Odd valiant*
Kenneth Wilfred Baker	*Knew the blinder freak*
Timothy Beaumont	*Hey! I'm mutant boot*
Peta Buscombe	*Obese bump act*
Robert Byron	*Terror by nob*
Timothy Jones	*Tiny homo jest*
William Coleridge	*I'm dire illegal cow*
Richard Ellenborough	*Horrible and cruel hog*
Diana Elles	*Lead aliens*
Charles Falconer	*Safer chancellor*
Josephine Farrington	*Joins hero if pregnant*
Derek Gladwin	*Darn wild geek*
John Keith Oliver	*Oh no! Hit evil jerk*
Patricia Hollis	*Political hairs*
Gloria Hopper	*Polar pig hero*
James Arthur Hope	*Jumps a hero hater*
Michael Levy	*My evil leach*
James Francis Lindsay	*Flimsy as rancid jeans*
Robert Hardy	*Dreary throb*
Andrew Lloyd Webber	*New drab lowly breed*
James Morrison	*I'm major snores*
Patricia Rawlings	*Warn racialist pig*
Nicholas Rootes	*Has corniest loo*

LABOUR POLITICIANS OF THE 1960S AND 1970S

Hugh Gaitskell	*Highgate skull*
Rt. Hon. James Callaghan PM	*Ah, small project hangman*
Harold Wilson	*Is darn hollow*
George Brown	*Ogre grew nob*
Denis Healey	*Hey! Lies dean*
Patrick Gordon Walker	*Polar-trekking coward*
Mister Tony Benn	*Try eminent snob*
Frank Cousins	*Sick arson fan*
Lord Gardinev	*Drivel dragon*
Anthony Greenwood	*Oh! Renowned gay, not!*
Barbara Castle	*Alabaster crab*
Gordon Walker	*God! Lower rank*
Michael Stewart	*White smart-alec*
Harry Nicholas	*Alas! Horny rich*
Len Williams	*Well, I'm snail*
Michael Foot	*I'm fool cheat*
Fred Peart	*Freed trap*
Roy Jenkins	*I jerk sonny*
Shirley Williams	*I'm a sly ill-wisher*
William Rodgers	*Wild male rigors*
Wedgwood Benn	*God! Now we bend!*
Dick Taverne	*Veteran dick*
Ron Hayward	*A horny draw*
Morgan Phillips	*Grim polish plan*
Tony Crosland	*Any cold snort*

LABOUR POLITICIANS OF THE 1980S AND 1990S

Tony Blair PM	*I'm Tory Plan B*
Gerald Kaufman	*Glum and a freak!*
Neil Kinnock	*I knock Lenin*
Peter Mandelson	*Lamented person*
Peter Shore	*Oh, Pesterer*
John Smith	*Him jot NHS*
Gordon Brown	*Wrong nob rod*
Margaret Beckett	*Met geek crab tart*
David Blunkett	*Dank butt devil*
Michael Meacher	*Him camera leech*
Robin Cook	*Mop biro conk*
Jack Cunningham	*Am chancing junk*
Harriet Harman	*Hi! A rant harmer*
John Prescott	*Chop jet snort*
Roy Hattersley	*Hey! Tarty loser*
Larry Whitty	*Tarty whirly*
Bryan Gould	*On ugly drab*
Jack Straw	*Jaw tracks*
Claire Short	*Harlot cries*
Stephen Byer	*Hey, bent press*
Frank Dobson	*Of darn knobs*
Donald Dewar	*Now dread lad*
Tom Sawyer	*Steamy row*
Denzel Davies	*Ends evil daze*
Eric Heffer	*Freer chief*

POLITICAL PARTIES

The Labour Party	*A bluer Tory path*
The Conservative Party	*Re-activate NHS poverty*
Liberal Democrats	*Creditable morals*
The Green Party	*The Energy Trap*
Scottish National Party	*Anti-social python tarts*
Plaid Cymru	*I'm duly crap*
Ulster Unionists	*In sluts routines*
The Referendum Party	*Tender, feathery rump*
The Democratic Unionist Party	*Dynamic teacher prostitution*
Social Democratic And Labour Party	*Brutally sad academic corporation*
The Workers Party	*Trashy power trek*
The Republican Socialist Party	*Attaches slippery lubrication*
The Progressive Unionist Party	*Universities pornography test*
Sinn Fein Party	*Infantry spine*
The Communist Party	*Traps the community*
The Socialist Party	*Yeah! Politics tarts!*
The Republican Party	*Breach planet purity*
The Democratic Party	*A mad, erotic crypt*
The Monster Raving Loony Party	*Oh! Government transitory play*
The UK Unionist Party	*Spirit tune thank you*
The Womens' Coalition	*Emotions now ethical*
The Christian Democrats	*Hard to trace in chemists*
The French Socialist Party	*Not the psychiatric flares*
The German Social Democrats	*Oh dear me! Galactic monsters!*
The Progressive Democrats	*Miss Pervert's good teacher!*

POLITICAL THINKERS & ECONOMISTS

Adam Smith	*Admit sham*
Rousseau	*Arouse us*
Mao Zedong	*Dogma zone*
Milton Friedman	*I flirt on madmen*
Aristotle	*Stale riot*
St Thomas Aquinas	*Am station squash*
Niccolo Machiavelli	*Civil mean alcoholic*
Thomas Hobbes	*Smash the boob*
Thomas Malthus	*Last sham mouth*
Edmund Burke	*Mud debunker*
Thomas Paine	*This ape moan*
Jeremy Bentham	*Betjeman rhyme*
Georg Wilhelm Friedrich Hegel	*Wriggle from high-heeled relic*
Charles Fourier	*Career flourish*
John Stuart Mill	*Small joint hurt*
Pierre Joseph Proudhon	*Jeer up posh heroin drop*
David Ricardo	*Odd arid vicar*
Friedrich Engels	*Fiend girls cheer*
Mohandas K Gandhi	*O man! Shaking dad*
Vladimir Ilyich Lenin	*Hid in lively criminal*
Adolf Hitler	*Harlot field*
Antonio Gramsci	*Orgasmic nation*
Friedrich August von Hayek	*Hard cheeky fatuous virgin*
Leon Walrus	*Slow neural*
John Maynard Keynes	*Many randy hen jokes*

WORLD LEADERS OF THE 1950S, 1960S AND 1970S

John Fitzgerald Kennedy	*Lazy jerk fended nothing*
President Richard Nixon	*In hard-core prints index*
Joseph Stalin	*Hapless joint*
Fidel Castro	*Docile farts*
Che Guevara	*A huge crave*
Nikita Khrushchev	*Shhh! Trick via nuke*
Souvanna Phouma	*A human soup nova*
Winston Churchill	*Churlish tin clown*
Lyndon Baines Johnson	*Ninny soon handles job*
Ngo Dinh Diem	*Hiding demon*
Rafael Trujillo	*A fuller jail rot*
Nguyen Cao Ky	*One yucky nag*
President Park Chung Hee	*The apprehending sucker*
Ferdinand Marcos	*Far rancid demons*
Aleksei N. Kosygin	*Ole! Gay kinkiness*
Nelson Rockefeller	*Serene Norfolk cell*
Leonid Brezhnev	*Bronze hen devil*
Gerald Ford	*Drag folder*
President Jimmy Carter	*Injected merry armpits*
Anwar El Sadat	*Dear Satan law*
Menachem Begin	*He beg manic men*
Harry S. Truman	*Run trash army*
President Eisenhower	*The weirdness pioneer*
Colonel Armas	*Local's moaner*
Chiang Kai-shek	*Aha! He's kicking!*

WORLD LEADERS OF THE 1980s & 1990s

President Clinton Of The USA	*To copulate he finds interns*
Hillary Clinton	*Only I can thrill*
President Boris Yeltsin	*Isn't one terribly pissed...*
Augusto Pinochet	*One top US CIA thug*
Ronald Reagan	*Arranged loan*
Saddam Hussein	*Human's sad side*
Martin Brian Mulroney	*I run my bar in Montreal*
Nelson Mandela	*Lean and solemn*
Mikhail Gorbachev	*Him bleak hog vicar*
George Herbert Walker Bush	*Huge beserk rebel warthog*
President Assad	*Sad pedestrians*
Yasser Arafat	*A safer astray*
Bertie Ahern	*Hen bite rear*
Maurice Bishop	*Some pubic hair*
Ferdinand Marcos	*Find sad romancer*
Pope John Paul The Second	*Loon epoch just happened*
Yitzhak Shamir	*I'm this hazy ark*
Francois Mitterand	*Mad strain of cretin*
Jean Marie Le Pen	*Jeer a penile man*
President Jacque Chirac	*Rejected anarchic quips*
Albert Reynolds	*Elderly snob rat*
Ayatollah Montazeri	*Hello, I am a Tarzan boy*
Ali Khamenei	*He like mania*
Mir Hossein Mousavi	*Ahem! Virus omission*
Slobodan Milosevic	*Visible loa condoms*

ARSENAL PLAYERS

Dennis Bergkamp	*Spank big red men*
David Seaman	*Damn save aid*
Martin Keown	*Woman tinker*
Emmanuel Petit	*Me penultimate*
Alan Ball	*All banal*
Liam Brady	*I'm drab lay*
Alan Sunderland	*Annulled Sandra*
Kenny Sansom	*Nanny smokes*
Alan Smith	*In ham list*
Tony Adams	*Sad toy man*
Lee Dixon	*Don exile*
David O'Leary	*A dry love aid*
Paul Merson	*Up loser man*
James Carter	*A Mars reject*
Joseph Mercer	*Chomps jeerer*
Mister Frank McLintock	*Film skin crack torment*
Charlie Buchan	*Ba! Church alien*
Alex James	*Sex jam ale!*
Charlie George	*Heroic leg rage*
Peter Storey	*Toy pesterer*
Marc Overmars	*Savor Mr. Cream*
Patrick Vieira	*Ice park trivia*
Nicholas Anelka	*Hosanna! Kill ace!*
Gilles Grimandi	*I'm all rigid legs*
Remi Garde	*A dire germ*

CHELSEA PLAYERS

Mr Ruud Gullit	*Turd mill guru*
Mister David Webb	*Beds brave dimwit*
Dennis Wise	*Snide swine*
Paul Elliot	*Ill lout ape*
Pat Nevin	*Pint nave*
Peter Bonetti	*Not better pie*
Ray Wilkins	*Is a wrinkly*
Peter Osgood	*Doorstep ego*
Eddie McCreadie	*Redeemed acidic*
Gianfranco Zola	*Nag fool czarina*
Roberto Di Matteo	*Mad beetroot riot*
Frank Sinclair	*In frisk carnal*
Mark Hughes	*Ugh! Mask her!*
Frank Leboeuf	*Foul-free bank*
Graeme Le Saux	*Lame sex argue*
Dan Petrescu	*Pant seducer*
Eddie Newton	*Denoted wine*
Player/Manager Gianluca Vialli	*Really plaguing a main cavalier*
Steve Clarke	*Sever tackle*
Michael Duberry	*Hey! I'm drab ulcer*
Tore Andre Flo	*Farted on role*
Kevin Hitchcock	*Thick oven chick*
Gustavo Poyet	*Soapy gut vote*
Celestine Babayaro	*Cease banality bore*
Dmitri Kharine	*I kid nit harmer*

LIVERPOOL PLAYERS

Paul Ince	*I clean up*
Jamie Redknapp	*Damp ape jerkin*
Steve McManaman	*TV man's enema cam*
Ian Rush	*Ha! Ruins!*
Alan Hansen	*Nasal henna*
Michael Owen	*Come in whale*
Robbie Fowler	*If low, rob beer*
Peter Thompson	*Honest pop term*
Gordon Wallace	*Large an' old cow*
Patrick Berger	*Grr! A peck biter*
Phil Neal	*Help! Pain!*
Jason McAteer	*A reject moans*
Peter Beardsley	*Player beds tree!*
John Aldridge	*Do hard jingle*
Steve Nicol	*Incest love*
Ray Houghton	*Ya! Thug honor*
Gary Gillespie	*I pillage 'greys'*
Ronnie Rosenthal	*He oral sinner...not!*
Bruce Grobbelaar	*Grab curable bore*
Dean Saunders	*An assured den*
Emlyn Hughes	*Ugly hen mesh*
Ian Callaghan	*Hail canal nag*
David Fairclough	*A godchild via fur*
Billy Stevenson	*Is slovenly bent*
Roger Hunt	*Grunt, hero*

MANCHESTER UNITED PLAYERS

Teddy Sheringham	*He'd shag dirty men*
Andrei Kanchelskis	*He's a lad in knickers*
Peter Davenport	*Poet and pervert*
Lee Sharpe	*He's a leper*
David Beckham	*Hacked bad vim*
Andy Cole	*Lady cone*
Dwight Yorke	*Right 'ow dyke*
Philip Neville	*I've nipple hill*
Gary Neville	*In every gall*
Eric Cantona	*Canine actor*
George Best	*Go get beers*
Ryan Giggs	*Angry gigs*
Roy Keane, Captain	*Inept ace ran Okay*
Peter Schmeichel	*Circle them sheep*
Bobby Charlton	*Holy brat on BBC*
Duncan Edwards	*Nude card's wand*
Denis Law	*Swine lad*
Paul Mc Grath	*Glum rat chap*
Bryan Robson	*Born bra nosy*
Johnny Carey	*Oh my! Rancidly jeer fiend*
Norman Whiteside	*Trained women*
Jesper Olsen	*Jeer pen loss*
Frank Stapleton	*Spank or flatten*
Nobby Stiles	*Bossily bent*
Gary Pallister	*Past girl layer*

TOTTENHAM HOTSPUR PLAYERS

Jimmy Greaves	*Germs may jive*
Martin Chivers	*I'm rich servant*
Chris Waddle	*Lad hid screw*
Steve Archibald	*Arch devil beast*
Gary Lineker	*Er? Kingly ear*
Jurgen Klinsmann	*Snarling men junk*
Mr Danny Blanchflower	*Warmly lynch 'n' fondle bra*
Alan Mullery	*Manly allure*
Steve Perryman	*Ya! Men perverts*
Gary Mabbott	*Ratty bag mob*
Paul Gascoigne	*Is language cop*
Justin Edinburgh	*Injured hung bits*
Darren Anderton	*Darn! Rear tendon*
Chris Armstrong	*Grrr! Manic shots*
Sol Campbell	*Compel balls*
Ramon Vega	*Grave moan*
Ossie Ardiles	*Is ladies' rose*
Ricardo Villa	*Livid car oral*
Martin Peters	*Printer's mate*
Dave Mackay	*Mad cave yak*
Les Ferdinand	*Slander fiend*
David Ginola	*A livid gonad*
Steffen Iverson	*Stern offensive*
Allan Nielson	*Lean lanolins*
Colin Calderwood	*Old-world cocaine*

AMERICAN BASKETBALL & BASEBALL TEAMS

The Chicago Bulls	*Locals huge bitch*
The Philadelphia Warriors	*Ha ha! Wild riot peripherals*
New York Knicks	*Wonky knickers*
Boston Celtics	*Colic snob test*
Los Angeles Lakers	*Large ankle losses*
The San Francisco Warriors	*Horrific crass Satan owner*
Baltimore Bullets	*All-time brute slob*
Milwaukee Bucks	*We suck bum alike*
Houston Rockets	*OK snot touchers*
Minneapolis Lakers	*Animal-like persons*
Seattle Supersonics	*Pretentious classes*
Washington Bullets	*Ha! Blows unsettling*
Syracuse Nationals	*No saucier analysts*
Fort Wayne Pistons	*Oops, nifty new star*
St Louis Hawks	*Silk washouts*
Detroit Pistons	*Pest distortion*
The Phoenix Suns	*Punish on the sex*
Boston Red Sox	*Next-door sobs*
Cincinnati Reds	*In rancid incest*
The Minnesota Twins	*Nastiest thin women*
Atlanta Braves	*Save banal tart*
Brooklyn Dodgers	*Odder knobs glory*
The Chicago Cubs	*Cough bitch aces*
Detroit Tigers	*Got dirtier set*
New York Yankees	*Keen Norway keys*

AMERICAN FOOTBALL TEAMS

Buffalo Bills	*Foul ball fibs*
Cincinnati Bengals	*Nice cannabis glint*
Cleveland Browns	*Bland novel screw*
Denver Broncos	*Nerd covers nob*
Indianapolis Colts	*Plain sadistic loon*
Kansas City Chiefs	*Nice shaky fascist*
Los Angeles Raiders	*Gorillas serenades*
Miami Dolphins	*His limp domain*
New England Patriots	*Slow and penetrating*
New York Jets	*Nosy wet jerk*
Pittsburgh Steelers	*Better ruthless pigs*
San Diego Chargers	*Gosh! Rancid grease!*
Seattle Seahawks	*Shake least sweat*
Atlanta Falcons	*Fatal snot canal*
Chicago Bears	*A rich bog case*
Dallas Cowboys	*Scold slob away*
Detroit Lions	*Dirtiest loon*
Green Bay Packers	*Nearby geek scrap*
Los Angeles Rams	*Large ass lemons*
Minnesota Vikings	*Is a stinking venom*
New Orleans Saints	*Raw non-essentials*
New York Giants	*Now gay stinker*
Philadelphia Eagles	*A hellish pig-lead ape*
Phoenix Cardinals	*Rich lad expansion*
Washington Redskins	*Drown skinniest shag*

BOXERS OF THE 1960S AND 1970S

Muhammad Ali	*Haul mad maim*
Cassius Clay	*Casual cissy*
Smokin' Joe Frazier	*I knife major zeros*
Sonny Liston	*So, ninny lost*
Henry Cooper	*Hey! Porn core*
Brian London	*In loon brand*
Karl Mildenburger	*Drunk liberal germ*
Eddie Duncan	*I danced nude*
Ruben Navarro	*An over-run bar*
Al Ford	*Of lard*
George Foreman	*Ogre fear gnome*
Larry Holmes	*Lo! Sly harmer*
Ken Buchanan	*Ban acne hunk*
Ismael Laguna	*I am a lush angel*
Alvaro Lopez	*Oval pro zeal*
Roberto Duran	*Terror abound*
Chris Finnegan	*Finch earnings*
Jorge Ahumada	*A huge road jam*
Bob Foster	*Boobs fret*
Oscar Bonavena	*Bravo! A acne son*
Joe Bugner	*Jeer on bug*
Rudiger Schmidtke	*The grim crude kids*
Emanuel Steward	*Mean sewer adult*
Eddie Marcelle	*Made elder lice*
Vincente Saldivar	*Vandalistic nerve*

BOXERS OF THE 1980S AND 1990S

Valerio Nali	*O, an evil liar*
Frank Bruno	*Fur knob ran*
Marlon Starling	*Snarling mortal*
Sugar Ray Leonard	*Rude organ salary*
Davey Moore	*Evade roomy*
Barry McGuigan	*Rub angry magic*
Marvin Hagler	*Ha! Grr! Evil man*
Lennox Lewis	*In well on sex*
Chris Eubank	*He suck brain*
Thomas Hearns	*Ha ha! Monsters*
Evander Holyfield	*Yeah! Devil fondler*
Wilfredo Gomez	*Deflower gizmo*
Asumah Nelson	*Oh! Sensual man*
Rocky Lockridge	*Bold grovery kick*
Alfredo Layne	*A early fondle*
Wilfred Benitez	*Finer weed blitz*
Dennis Andries	*Darn! Denies sin*
Mike Tyson	*Sit! Monkey!*
Mike Spinks	*Kiss me pink*
Llyod Honeyghan	*Lonely handy hog*
Kevin Howard	*I've handwork*
Prince Naseem Hamed	*Serene damp machine*
Salvador Sanchez	*Oh! Vandals crazes*
Buster Douglas	*Absolute drugs*
Carl Williams	*Ill racism law*

ENGLAND FOOTBALL PLAYERS OF THE 1960S AND 1970S

Raymond Wilkins	*Is womanly drink*
Norbert Stiles	*Brittle snores*
David Watson	*Did Satan vow*
Ramon Wilson	*Now moral sin*
Gordon Banks	*Dragon knobs*
Thomas Beattle	*That mole beast!*
Bobby Moore	*Obey orb mob*
Trevor Brooking	*Overt knob rigor*
Ronald Clayton	*Na! Lady control*
Allan Clarke	*Call ale rank*
Trevor Cherry	*Fat jersey elf*
Michael Bailey	*Ha! Lay imbecile*
Raymond Clemence	*Recycle demon man*
Peter Barnes	*Preen breast*
Bryan Douglas	*Adorably snug*
George Eastham	*Hates mega ogre*
Ronald Flowers	*Darn fowl loser*
James Greaves	*Severe gas jam*
Barry Bridges	*Bribery drags*
Emlyn Hughes	*Mushy hen leg*
Geoff Hurst	*Hog stuffer*
Roy McFarland	*Crony lad farm*
Alan Mullery	*Manly allure*
Martin Peters	*Printer's mate*
Ronald Springett	*Darn piglet snort*

ENGLAND FOOTBALL PLAYERS OF THE 1980S AND 1990S

Vivian Anderson	*Nova sin invader*
David Armstrong	*Odd vagrant's rim*
Stuart Pearce	*Pure castrate*
Gareth Southgate	*Gosh! Eat huge tart*
David Batty	*Tidy a bad TV*
Terry Butcher	*Cherry butter*
Luther Blisset	*Sluttish rebel*
Peter Shilton	*The snot peril*
Trevor Francis	*Con river farts*
Alan Shearer	*Hear Arsenal*
Paul Mariner	*Remap urinal*
Gary Pallister	*Large spy trial*
Mark Chamberlain	*Hack Mr Lamebrain*
Kenneth Sansom	*Hasn't seen monk*
Trevor McGregor Steven	*Erect TV governor germs*
Michael Stevens	*Enslave chemist*
Philip Thompson	*Shh! No Pimp pilot*
Christopher Waddle	*Horrid lewd patches*
Desmond Walker	*Mad-keen worlds*
Christopher Woods	*Hero drops this cow*
Ian Wright	*Hi! Gin wart*
Dion Dublin	*Loud din bin*
Nigel Martyn	*Tiny mangler*
Graham Le Saux	*Ugh! A sex alarm*
Paul Scholes	*Slouch leaps*

ENGLISH & SCOTTISH PREMIER TEAMS

Manchester United	*A hide encrustment*
Liverpool FC	*Pelvic floor*
Arsenal FC	*A serf clan*
Tottenham Hotspur	*Ho-Hum! Potent tarts*
Newcastle United	*Lunatics weed net*
Chelsea	*Leaches*
Nottingham Forest	*Fortnight team, son*
Blackburn Rovers	*Lark! Overruns BBC*
Leeds United	*Let's die nude*
West Ham United	*Thud swine team*
Everton	*Over net*
Aston Villa	*Vital loans*
Sheffield Wednesday	*Hey! Lads sniffed weed*
Southampton	*Shot-put moans*
Wimbledon	*Bowel mind*
Coventry City	*Covet tiny cry*
Leicester City	*Electric Yetis*
Celtic Football Club	*Foul blob cell tactic*
Glasgow Rangers	*Gargle wrong ass*
Aberdeen	*A beer end*
Motherwell Football Club	*Hell! Total cruel bomb foul*
Hearts	*Haters*
Dundee United	*Unedited nude*
Kilmarnock	*Normal kick*
Hibernian FC	*Fine inch bra*

ENGLISH CRCKETERS OF 1960S & 1970S

Dennis Amiss	*I'm sinned ass*
Trevor Bailey	*Retrieval boy*
Ken Barrington	*Bonking ranter*
Geoffrey Boycott	*Effect booty orgy*
Brian Close	*Basic loner*
Mister Geoff Griffin	*Offering stiff grime*
Tom Graveney	*Got everyman*
Ray Illingworth	*I worry all night*
Mr Allan Knott	*Tart man knoll*
Peter May	*Mate prey*
Alec Bedser	*Bled crease*
Leg-break bowler John Snow	*Well-worn jerk, he's a bog nob*
Brian Statham	*I bash tart man*
Fred Truman	*Remand turf*
Johnny Wardle	*Lend horny jaw*
All-rouder Ted Dexter	*Extended a dull terror*
Batsman Colin Cowdrey	*Can't considerably mow*
Mister John Edrich	*Inject horrid mesh*
Tony Grieg	*Ginger toy*
Derek Pringle	*Red leper king*
Keith Fletcher	*The cheek flirt*
Mike Brearley	*Limey breaker*
Ian Chappell	*Na! Cheap pill*
Batsman Greg Chappell	*Gamblers can't help gap*
Bob Woolmer	*Bore low mob*
Lawrence Rowe	*New career low*

ENGLISH CRICKETERS OF THE 1980s & 1990s

Michael Atherton	*Came In The Harlot*
Ian Botham	*Oh man! I bat*
Mike Gatting	*Giant gem kit*
Graham Gooch	*Macho hog rag*
David Gower	*Do drag view*
Jack Russell	*Call us jerks*
Alec Stewart	*Claret sweat*
Derek Underwood	*Do reworked nude*
Bob Willis	*I blow bills*
Allan Lamb	*Banal mall*
Bill Athey	*Yell habit*
Graham Dilley	*Him large lady*
Dennis Lillie	*Ill senile din*
Rodney Marsh	*Horny dreams*
Tim Robinson	*I'm in snob rot*
Richard Ellison	*Ill hardcore sin*
Chris Broad	*So rich drab*
Gladstone Small	*Let's slag old man*
Steve Waugh	*He waves gut*
Graham Thorpe	*Ha ha! Germ port*
Craig McDermott	*I'm cool germ tract*
Shane Warne	*She ran anew*
Captain Nasser Hussain	*A piranha's satanic suns*
Dean Headley	*Day he leaned*
Angus Fraser	*Arrange fuss*

ENGLISH FOOTBALL TEAMS

Middlesbrough	*Huge bird's mold*
Bolton Wanderers	*Owned nobler star*
Southend United	*This nude-to-nude*
Sheffield United	*Die! Fit nude flesh*
Manchester City	*My! Cretin cheats!*
Colchester United	*Consulted heretic*
Leyton Orient	*Enter tiny loo*
Sunderland	*Larded nuns*
Norwich City	*Tiny rich cow*
Watford Football Club	*Flout fatal crowd blob*
Crystal Palace	*Stale clay carp*
Swindon Town	*Down-town sin*
West Bromwich Albion	*Oh wow! Nice brat limbs*
Hereford United FC	*Horrid nude effect*
Wolverhampton Wanderers	*He's worn pavement warlord*
Derby County	*Yo! Trendy club*
Ipswich Town	*Isn't cow whip*
Queens Park Rangers	*Grr! Snap queer sneak*
Tranmere Rovers	*Stern rear mover*
Oldham Athletic	*Ahem! Total child*
Bristol City	*Stoic trilby*
Portsmouth	*Rum hotspot*
Oxford United	*No! Odd fixture*
Notts County	*No! Nutty Scot*
Portvale	*Love trap*

FAMOUS GOLFERS

Nick Faldo	*A fond lick*
Tiger Woods	*I'd worst ego*
Bobby Jones	*Bye! Snob job*
Johnny Miller	*A novice pry*
Mark McNulty	*Clammy trunk*
Payne Stewart	*Sweaty parent*
Gary Wolstenholme	*Well, the moron's gay*
Colin Montgomerie	*Grim emotion clone*
Severiano Ballesteros	*Resolves elaborate sin*
Ian Woosnam	*A wino moans*
Ronan Rafferty	*Faery ran front*
Bernhard Langer	*Her barren gland*
Greg Norman	*Grog manner*
Curtis Strange	*Gastric unrest*
Laura Davies	*A devil's aura*
Ernie Els	*Sneer lie*
Fred Couples	*Rescued flop*
Philip Tataurangi	*Aha! Ritual pint pig*
Walter Hage	*Weather gal*
Arnold Palmer	*Me planar lord*
Gene Sarazen	*Sane gezer? Na!*
Bruce Lietzke	*Ice beer klutz*
Sam Snead	*A madness*
Phil Mickelson	*Help! I'm in locks*
Lanny Wadkins	*Walk! Sad ninny*

FEMALE ATHLETES & SPORT STARS

Michelle Smith	*I'm the slim lech*
Larissa Latynina	*Nail art analysis*
Nancy Kerrigan	*In cranky rage*
Tonya Harding	*Had tiny groan*
Evelyn Ashford	*Heavy fondlers*
Yvonne Murray	*Vary money run*
Sara Simeoni	*Mission area*
Florence Griffith Joyner	*I reject horny fling offer*
Chen Yueling	*Nice ugly hen*
Jackie Joyner Kersee	*Yankee jerks rejoice!*
Petra Felke	*Keep falter*
Martina Hellman	*Alarm ninth male*
Louise Ritter	*Is torture lie?*
Debbie Flintoff King	*If fiend felt big knob*
Yordanka Donkova	*OK on a randy vodka*
Olga Bondarenko	*A broken gonadal*
Joan Benoit	*A bone joint*
Tatyana Samolenko	*A total sneaky moan*
Miss Paula Ivan	*Sup main saliva*
Olga Bryzgina	*A zany girl bog*
Ilona Slupianek	*OK, up alien snail*
Sabine John	*She join ban*
Francie Larrieu Smith	*Christ! Remain failure*
Joyce Smith	*Chemist joy*
Yelena Nikolayeva	*Naive loyal Yankee*

FEMALE TENNIS PLAYERS OF THE 1960S AND 1970S

Billie Jean King	*Kneel in big jail*
Virginia Wade	*Raid a viewing*
Chris Evert	*Itch server*
Tracy Austin	*In saucy tart*
Hana Mandlikova	*Ha! I'm an OK vandal*
Evonne Goolagong Cawley	*Now gave colon genealogy*
Kristy Pigeon	*It pesky groin*
Peaches Bartkowicz	*Zebra with peacocks*
Pam Shriver	*Prim shaver*
Greer Stevens	*Regent serves*
Rosie Casals	*Alias scores*
Judy Tegart Dalton	*Not tart lady judge*
Diane Balestrat	*Liberated Satan*
Margaret Court	*Great court arm*
Sylvia Hanika	*Hi! Saliva yank*
Regina Marsikova	*OK, I'm a sin ravager*
Sue Barker	*Break user*
Rosalyn Fairbank-Nideffer	*Friskier affordable nanny*
Mirna Jausovec	*Am junior's cave*
Bettina Bunge	*Been bit gaunt*
Betsy Nagelsen	*Bent gay lenses*
Helga Mastoff	*Fat flog shame*
Kerry Melville Reid	*My! Killer deliverer*
Gladys Heldman	*Mangled shy lad*
Patti Hogan	*Oath taping*

FEMALE TENNIS PLAYERS OF THE 1980S AND 1990S

Steffi Graf	*Stiffer fag*
Arantxa Sanchez Vicario	*Is an arch Nazi excavator*
Martina Navratilova	*Variant rival to a man*
Larisa Neiland	*An airline's lad*
Kimiko Date	*OK media kit*
Mary Pierce	*Racy empire*
Natalia Zvereva	*Leave via Tarzan*
Monica Seles	*Smiles on ace*
Lori McNeil	*I'm ill crone*
Jennifer Capriati	*I fart in jeer panic*
Martina Hingis	*Ha! I'm straining*
Gabriela Sabatini	*Insatiable airbag*
Lindsey Davenport	*Evidently sad porn*
Meredith McGrath	*Ditch the germ arm*
Anna Kournikova	*U an nirvana, kook*
Gigi Fernandez	*Fingering daze*
Manuela Maleeva Fragniere	*I am a venereal funeral game*
Mary Joe Fernandez	*Framed on zany jeer*
Helen Sukova	*Have one sulk!*
Venus Williams	*Values slim wins*
Jelena Dokic	*Nice lad joke*
Sabine Appelmans	*An impassable pen*
Zina Garrison	*Arizona grins*
Gigi Fernandez	*Fingering daze*
Conchita Martinez	*Not a citizen charm*

FOOTBALL GROUNDS

White Hart Lane	*The alien wrath*
Highbury Stadium	*Ugh! I'm a dirty bush*
Old Trafford, Manchester	*Death cradles from front*
Villa Park Ground	*OK! Rival drug plan*
Nou Camp	*Cup moan*
Celtic Park	*Carp tickle*
Delle Alpi, Italy	*Lately laid pile*
Anfield	*Idle fan*
Ibrox Park Ground	*I drug ark box porn*
Wembley Stadium	*I am sweetly dumb*
Hampden Park	*Eh? Damp prank*
Giuseeppe Meazza Ground	*Unzipped - a gruesome gaze*
Olympia-stadion	*My isolation pad*
San Paolo	*Soap loan*
Rose Bowl Ground	*Undo slob grower*
Mario Filho	*Hi! I farm loo*
Olympico Ground	*O my! Drooling cup*
Morumbi	*Biro mum*
The Dell Ground	*Noted drug hell*
Upton Park	*Kaput porn*
Goodison Park	*Poison drag OK*
St. James Park	*A jerk's stamp*
Maine Road	*I am a drone*
Centenario	*An erection*
Monumental, Argentina	*Man-eating lout manner*

FOOTBALL MANAGERS

Alex Ferguson	*Flaxen rogues*
George Graham	*Meager hog rag*
Kevin Keegan	*Vain 'ken' geek*
Kenny Daglish	*Dinghy ankles*
Terry Venables	*Try eleven bras*
Matt Busby	*Batty bums*
Arsene Wegner	*New sheer rage*
Jackie Charlton	*Catch nail joker*
Mister Bobby Robson	*Riot bombs snobbery*
Graeme Souness	*A gruesomeness*
Bob Paisley	*Pie slob bay*
Brian Clough	*Rich loan bug*
Josef 'Sepp' Herberger	*Erg! Prefer's sheep jobs*
Alf Ramsey	*False army*
William Shankly	*Milk in hallways*
Harry Redknapp	*Err... drank happy*
Franz Beckenbauer	*Ban funk car breeze*
Herbert Chapman	*Ha! Temper branch*
Wim Jansen	*In news jam*
Valeri Lobanovsky	*Looks vain bravely*
Karl Rappan	*Pal ran park*
Arthur Rowe	*Ow! Hurt rear*
Graham Taylor	*Ha! Gray mortal*
Tele Santana	*A sane talent*
Glenn Hoddle	*Held long end*

FORMULA ONE DRIVERS OF THE 1960S AND 1970S

Mario Andretti	*I'm retardation*
Rene Arnoux	*O! Axe runner*
Lorenzo Bandini	*Inbred Nazi loon*
Jean-Pierre Beltoise	*Jeer bestial pioneer*
Vittorio Brambilla	*Ballroom trivia bit*
Francois Cevert	*Covers nicer fat*
Patrick Depailler	*Killed carp pirate*
Tony Brooks	*Yo! Rots Knob*
James Hunt	*Human jest*
Innes Ireland	*Alien's dinner*
Peter Gethin	*The ripe gent*
Bruce McLaren	*Cancer rumble*
Stirling Moss	*Lost grim sins*
Gunnar Nilsson	*Na! Running loss*
Ronnie Peterson	*Represent onion*
Didier Pironi	*Oi! In dire drip*
Clay Regazzoni	*No! A grizzly ace*
Carlos Reutemann	*Na! A cruel monster*
Peter Revson	*Perverse ton*
Pedro Rodriguez	*Or rude dog prize*
Keke Rosberg	*Geek brokers*
Ludovico Scarfiotti	*A circuit fool's divot*
Jody Schechter	*Shh! Cry, do eject!*
Gilles Villeneuve	*Use evil levelling*
Jackie Stewart	*Is water jacket*

FORMULA ONE DRIVERS OF THE 1980S AND 1990S

Michele Alboreto	*Hello! Erotic beam*
Rubens Barichello	*Burns heroic labels*
Martin Brundle	*Mind blunt rear*
David Coulthard	*Do valid car thud*
Ayrton Senna	*Anyone rants*
Emerson Fittipaldi	*Ironfisted pit male*
Andrea de Cesaris	*A dearer acidness*
Thierry Boutsen	*Sure hit rent-boy*
Mister Johnny Herbert	*I'm horny jest brethren*
Damon Hill	*Na! Him doll!*
Eddie Irvine	*I envied ride*
Jan Magnussen	*Snug jeans man*
Nigel Mansell	*All single men*
Mika Salo	*I am koalas*
Alessandro Nannini	*Insane inland arson*
Oliver Panis	*Is evil apron*
Jonathan Palmer	*Napalm jet honor*
Riccardo Patrese	*Reads erotic crap*
Nelson Piquet	*Eloquent spin*
Alain Prost	*I star on lap*
Michael Schumacher	*Much malice – he crash!*
Ralf Schumacher	*Fuel crash charm*
Jos Verstappen	*Vast porn jeeps*
Derek Warwick	*Wreak kid crew*
Heinz Harald Frentzen	*He earn frazzled ninth*

INTERNATIONAL FOOTBALL TEAMS

Standard Liege	*Dread genitals*
Paris Saint-Germain	*Repairing Satanism*
Sparta Prague	*Ape sugar trap*
River Plate	*Viper alert*
Red Star Belgrade	*Retarded garbles*
Atletico Madrid	*Omitted radical*
Boca Juniors	*Sour jacobin*
Barcelona	*A clear nob*
Kiev Dynamo	*I'm nova dyke*
Marseille	*Real slime*
Anderlecht	*Leach trend*
Ajax Amsterdam	*Jam a sex-mad rat*
Bayern Munich FC	*Farce in my bunch*
PSV Eindhoven Football Club	*Blood vol-au-vents flip bench*
Sporting Clube	*Blustering cop*
Shooting Stars	*Rations ghosts*
Athletic Bilbao	*Liable to a bitch*
Monchengladbach	*Ha! Damn bog clench*
Steaua Bucharest	*Acute trash abuse*
Croatia Zagreb	*I abrogate Czar*
IFK Gothenburg	*Fight knob urge*
Internazionale Milan	*In animal latrine zone*
Eintracht Frankfurt	*Thank current tariff*
Moscow Spartak	*Worst camp soak*
Borussia Dortmund	*Sod us brain-rot mud*

INTERNATIONAL FOOTBALL PLAYERS OF THE 1960S & 70S

Reinaldo Zico	*Ironical doze*
George Sideris	*Soggier desire*
Gerd Muller	*Lured Mr leg*
Roberto Rivelino	*Boo! In evil terror*
Antonis Antoniadis	*No! An idiot Satan sin*
Dieter Muller	*Met idle ruler*
Carlos Bianchi	*I anarchic slob*
Erwin Van Den Berg	*Raving new bender*
Dud Georgesu	*Dug rude egos*
Romeo Benetti	*Boot'em entire*
Ernie Brandts	*Inserted bran*
Mario Kempes	*Is a meek romp*
Rob Rensenbrink	*Born inner berks*
Teofillio Cubillas	*Bull loo facilities*
Mister Johannes Neeskens	*This jerk's enema nonsense*
Daniel Passarella	*Lad seals airplane*
Roberto Bettega	*Greet boob treat*
Daniel Bertoni	*Brain deletion*
Renato Zaccarelli	*Create Nazi collar*
Rainer Bonhof	*Nab for heroin*
Sepp Maier	*Aimer's rep*
Klaus Fischer	*Lick us afresh*
Hans Muller	*Ah, Mr. sullen*
Mister Hans Krankl	*Sank Kremlin trash*
Piet Wildschut	*Wide pitch slut*

INTERNATIONAL FOOTBALL PLAYERS OF THE 1980S & 1990S

Marco Van Basten	*Crab Satan venom*
Hugo Sanchez	*Hug cash zone*
Fernando Gomes	*Semen of dragon*
Karl Heinz Rummenigge	*Energize ramming hulk*
Niko Anastopoulos	*Soak utopian loons*
Martin McGaughey	*Charming team guy*
Toni Polster	*Toilets porn*
Peter Houtman	*Oh! Mutant peer*
Georgi Slarkov	*Risk aggro love*
Dorin Mateut	*No! Tedium rat*
Roger Milla	*A grime roll*
Salvatore Schillacci	*Allocates chic rivals*
Diego Maradonna	*O dear! Main gonad*
Ronald Koeman	*A damn OK loner*
Claudio Caniggia	*I aid gaga council*
Thomas Berthold	*Mad hot brothels*
Lothar Matthaus	*Ho-hum! Tart atlas*
Andreas Brehme	*Baseman herder*
Roberto Baggio	*I abort ogre bog*
Kevin Sheedy	*He's dyke vine*
Roberto Carlos	*Slob coat error*
Ricardo Gomes	*Orgasmic doer*
Valderrama	*Dream larva*
Michel Platini	*In ethical limp*
Paulo Rossi	*Sailor soup*

INTERNATIONAL CRICKET PLAYERS

Abdul Qadir	*Ribald quad*
Neil Adcock	*Naked colic*
Terry Alderman	*Learned martyr*
Curtly Ambrose	*My brutal score*
Lala Amarnath	*Ah, natal alarm*
Mohammad Azharuddin	*Hazard on humid madam*
Eddie Barlow	*A weirdo bled*
Richie Benaud	*Hi! Buried acne*
Allan Border	*Drear no-ball*
Martin Crowe	*Now crime rat*
Michael Holding	*Oh! I'm angel child*
Mister Imran Khan	*Na! I'm harm stinker*
Douglas Jardine	*Slag dead junior*
Anil Kumble	*Menial bulk*
Dennis Lillee	*Ill sinned lie*
Rodney Marsh	*Horny dreams*
Graeme Pollock	*Legal coke romp*
Mike Proctor	*Me root prick*
Barry Richards	*Carry bird rash*
Richie Richardson	*Irish record chain*
Ravi Shastri	*I ravish rats*
Bobby Simpson	*Snob bimbo spy*
Mister Mark Taylor	*Try immoral streak*
Sachin Tendulkar	*Na! Ethical drunks*
Courtney Walsh	*What curly ones*

JOCKEYS AND SHOWJUMPERS

Sir Lester Piggott	*Glitter pig tosser*
Charlie Swan	*Rascal whine*
Frankie Dettori	*Rent idiot freak*
Katherine Burdsall	*Dull sneakier brat*
Alwin Schockemohle	*Oh hell! Sick mean cow*
David Broome	*I'm brave dodo*
Pat Koechlin-Smythe	*Impotent shaky lech*
Frank Chapot	*Fat porn hack*
Harvey Smith	*This very ham*
Peter Robeson	*Prone to beers*
Malcolm Pyrah	*Ha! Calmly romp*
John Whitaker	*Ha! Now hit jerk*
Nick Skelton	*Silent knock*
Caroline Bradley	*Nice balder royal*
William Steinkraus	*I'm saintlike walrus*
Hans Gunter Winkler	*Threw snarling nuke*
Derek Ricketts	*Erect Trek kids*
Lionel Dunning	*Lone idling nun*
Jed O'Dwyer	*Dowdy jeer*
Graziano Mancinelli	*Canonize animal girl*
Raimondo d'Inzeo	*Main indoor doze*
Hartwig Steenken	*We threaten kings*
Michael Matz	*I'm match zeal*
Kathy Kusner	*Hearty skunk*
Dawn Palethorpe	*Hated power-plan*

MALE ATHLETES

Sebastian Coe	*Obese Satanic*
Alexei Urmanov	*O! A vixen mauler*
Linford Christie	*Flirted in choirs*
Anders Holmertz	*Lather Mrs. Dozen*
Alexander Popov	*A proven dope lax*
Mr Kevin Young	*My evoking run*
Dennis Mithchell	*Hell! Incest mind*
Colin Jackson	*Can join locks*
Michael Bates	*Sham celibate*
Carl Lewis	*A ill screw*
Kirk Baptiste	*Skip bike tart*
Steve Lewis	*Sweet evils*
Phil Edwards	*Rash lewd dip*
Frankie Fredericks	*Fear fried knickers*
Richard Chelimo	*Horrid chemical*
Kriss Akabussi	*Basis irks skua*
David Wilkie	*Add evil kiwi*
Roger Kingdom	*Grr! OK ego mind*
Bob Beamon	*A bone bomb*
Hassiba Boulmerka	*Abolish Mark's bean*
Michael Marsh	*Ha! Slime charm*
Quincy Watts	*Quit nasty WC*
Mike Conley	*Monkey lice*
Daley Thompson	*A! Dopes monthly*
Sergei Litinov	*Ego isn't virile*

MALE TENNIS PLAYERS OF THE 1960S AND 1970S

John 'The Brat' McEnroe	*Oh man! The born reject*
Tony Roche	*Hey! Rot con*
The Star Jimmy Connors	*Christ! Monster man joy*
John Newcombe	*Chew on men job*
Tom Okker	*Kook term*
Stan Smith	*Sham stint*
Roger Taylor	*Orgy relator*
Ray Moore	*Romeo ray*
Pierre Barthes	*Ripe bear trash*
Marty Riessen	*Messy terrain*
Arthur Ashe	*Has hurt ear*
Manuel Orantes	*Rue on stale man*
Guillermo Vilas	*Vulgar oil slime*
Bjorn Borg	*Grr! Nob job*
Eddie Dibbs	*Bedside bid*
Ilie Nastase	*A! It's a senile*
Brian Gottfried	*Brain-rot fidget*
Roscoe Tanner	*Rot resonance*
Janes Kodas	*Joke ass den*
Dick Stockton	*Don tick-tocks*
Gene Mayer	*Enemy gear*
Jose-Luis Clerc	*Jello circuses*
Vitas Gerulaitis	*Evil Sagittarius*
Janes Kodes	*As joke ends*
Ken Rosewall	*Slower ankle*

MALE TENNIS PLAYERS OF THE 1980S AND 1990S

Pete Sampras	*Ape stampers*
Andre Agassi	*Grass: an aide*
Tim Henman	*Me thin man*
Greg Rusedski	*Rugged kisser*
Michael Stich	*This chemical*
Richard Fromberg	*Grrr! If macho bred*
Nicholas Pereira	*Airplane heroics*
Patrick Rafter	*Rap after trick*
Yevgeny Kafelnikov	*Envy geek, OK vain fly*
Andrei Olhovskiy	*Oh no! A risky devil*
Andrew Foster	*Worsened fart*
Goran Ivanisevic	*Vain cave origins*
Boris Becker	*Sober bicker*
Stefan Edberg	*Gent fears bed*
Kenneth Carlsen	*Na! Kernal stench*
Guy Forget	*True foggy*
Petr Korda	*Parked rot*
Markus Zoecke	*OK sucker maze*
Chuck Adams	*Ha! Duck scam*
Todd Martin	*Don dim tart*
Sergi Bruguera	*Grr! I abuse urge*
Michael Chang	*High calm acne*
Jeremy Bates	*Beer majesty*
Mark Goellner	*Lone lark germ*
Richard Krychek	*Hark! Cherry dick!*

RUGBY CLUBS

Huddersfield Giants	*Huge islands drifted*
Warrington Wolves	*Wow! Overt snarling*
Whitehaven Warriors	*A harsh interview row*
Widnes Vikings	*New diving kiss*
Wigan Warriors	*Rigor in Warsaw*
Workington Town	*Wrong kit? Not now!*
Barrow Border Raiders	*Drabber warrior doer*
Batley Bulldogs	*Blast dull bogey*
Carlisle Border Raiders	*Ill drab drearier scores*
Castleford Tigers	*Strategic folders*
Dewsbury Rams	*Buy warm dress*
Doncaster Dragons	*Tranced organ sods*
Featherstone Rovers	*Heretofore servants*
Hull Kingston Rovers	*Hi! Overstrung knols*
Keighley Cougars	*Ugh! Creakily egos*
Lancashire Lynx	*Na! Lynch sex liar*
Leigh Centurions	*Cheering in louts*
London Broncos	*No! Con snob Lord*
Paris Saint Germain	*Repairing Satanism*
Prescot Panthers	*Presents hot carp*
Rochdale Hornets	*Race on threshold*
Salford Reds	*Flared dross*
Sheffield Eagles	*He feed slag flies*
Swinton Lions	*Now on sin list*
Wakefield Trinity	*I dwarflike entity*

RUGBY PLAYERS

Kevin Walters	*Knew evil star*
Will Carling	*Win call-girl*
Tevita Vaikona	*A vain ovate kit*
Dean Hanger	*Na! Hard gene*
Ray Waring	*A wary grin*
Andrew Farrell	*Rarer fan dwell*
Darren Smith	*Smarter hind*
Dean Bell	*Ale blend*
Clayton Friend	*Fondly a cretin*
Stephen Kearney	*Rank teeny sheep*
Craig Polla-Mounter	*Cool April argument*
Ricky Stewart	*Is tarty wreck*
Brad Fittler	*Flatter bird*
Martin Offiah	*I month affair*
Mister Glenn Lazarus	*Sure-smelling Tarzan*
Jonathan Davies	*Na! Have sad joint*
Quentin Pongia	*Na! Pong in quiet*
Paul Osborne	*Usable porno*
Steve Walters	*Last wet serve*
Shaun Edwards	*Ha! Draws nudes*
Garry Schofield	*Glory if chased*
Bobby Goulding	*God! Buying blob!*
Jason Williams	*Now I jam ill ass*
Wendell Sailor	*Well idle arson*
Brett Mullins	*Isn't Mr. Bullet*

SCOTTISH FOOTBALL PLAYERS

Gordon Durie	*Ruin odd ogre*
Ally McCoist	*Local mystic*
Football Player John Hughes	*Hallelujah! Y-fronts bog hope*
Mark Humphries	*Hmm! I pure shark*
Gerard Creaney	*Dry career range*
Brian McLaughlin	*Hung cranial limb*
Martin Hayes	*Man hysteria*
James Leighton	*Join slag theme*
Scott Mackensie	*Semantic socket*
Derek Crawford	*Red crowd freak*
Ian Ferguson	*Unsafe groin*
Gary McSwegan	*Am screwy gang*
Rodney Patterson	*Dopey non-starter*
Michael Stevens	*The manic vessel*
Kevin McGowne	*Known gem vice*
Andrew Morgan	*Now a darn germ*
David Nicholson	*No! Vain child sod*
Paul Patterson	*Prenatal spout*
Alexander Robertson	*External broad snore*
Mister John Walker	*Mother-in-law jerks*
Mark Andrew McLean	*Damn! Wreck real man*
Charles Nicholas	*SOS! Anarchic hell*
Andrew Payton	*Now randy tape*
Stephen Fulton	*Hunt tense flop*
Duncan Shearer	*Rash endurance*

AMERICAN ARTISTS

Carl Andre	*Carnal red*
Susan Hiller	*Linear slush*
Alexander Calder	*Relax! Red acne lad*
Mary Cassatt	*Ya! Tarts scam*
Judy Chicago	*Juicy cod hag*
Robert Gober	*Be bog terror*
Richard Diebenkorn	*Abhorred inner dick*
Thomas Eakins	*Eh? OK Satanism*
Jacob Epstein	*Job's patience*
Lyonnel Feininger	*Fine leering nylon*
Eric Fischl	*Fish cleric*
Philip Guston	*Ho! Piping slut*
Keith Haring	*The hair king*
Winslow Homer	*Now slim whore*
Edward Hopper	*Powder her pad*
Julian Schnabel	*China Bull jeans*
Roy Lichtenstein	*No! It isn't lechery!*
Laszlo Moholy-Nagy	*Oh my! Lazy loon slag*
Jean-Michel Basquiat	*Inequitable cash jam*
Robert Rauschenberg	*Grr! He bounce breast*
James Rosenquist	*Square joint mess*
Susan Rothenberg	*No! Breasts hunger*
Dorothea Tanning	*No! Hated ignorant*
Andy Warhol	*Ha! Worn lady*
Andrew Wyeth	*New wry death*

BRITISH ARTISTS

Craigie Aitchison	*I is aching erotica*
Michael Andrews	*New medical rash*
Terry Atkinson	*Stinker on tray*
Gillian Ayres	*A grisly alien*
Aubrey Vincent Beardsley	*An everyday insect rubble*
William Blake	*I'll awake limb*
Edward Burne-Jones	*Nude jobs wanderer*
Sir Anthony Caro	*Honorary sin act*
Leonora Carrington	*Arrogant inner cool*
Patrick Caulfield	*Practical fuel kid*
Helen Chadwick	*Whacked lichen*
John Constable	*Snatch lone job*
Dame Laura Knight	*Harangue dim talk*
Dame Elizabeth Frink	*Feminize her bad talk*
Thomas Gainsborough	*Housing bathroom gas*
Richard Hamilton	*Ditch normal hair*
Nicholas Hilliard	*In a cold Irish hall*
William Holman Hunt	*Ill mouth annal whim*
Sir Edwin Landseer	*Rained wilderness*
Frederic Leighton	*Grr! Deficient hole*
Sir John Everett Millais	*Jails the virile monster*
Dante Gabriel Rossetti	*Obliterated arse sting*
Sir Stanley Spencer	*Plays secret sinner*
Joseph Mallord William Turner	*Hello, limp wristed ram journal*
Henry Wallis	*Swinery hall*

CLASSICAL COMPOSERS

Ludwig Van Beethoven	*Loved having new tube*
Wolfgang Amadeus Mozart	*Zealous, warm 'n' mad faggot*
Michael Tippet	*He tactile pimp*
Richard Wagner	*Grr! Inward ache*
Giuseppe Verdi	*Give rude pipes*
Sir Franz Joseph Haydn	*Shh! Defy porn jar Nazis*
Johann Sebastian Bach	*Aha! Enchantin' bass job!*
George Frideric Handel	*Dredge large fine choir*
George Philipp Teleman	*Telephone pilgrimage*
Antonio Vivaldi	*Invalid ovation*
Claudio Monteverdi	*Demoniac devil rout*
William Byrd	*I'm wally bird*
Johannes Brahms	*Hash job manners*
Pyotr Tchaikovsky	*OK, vast itchy porky*
Claude Debussy	*Seduce lady sub*
Sergei Rachmaninov	*I'm arsenic hangover*
Sergei Prokofiev	*OK if I go perverse?*
George Gershwin	*Ginger sewer hog*
Aaron Copland	*Carol on panda*
Georges Bizet	*Bigot's geezer*
Leonard Bernstein	*No! Latrines bender*
Richard Strauss	*Is crud star rash*
Igor Stravinsky	*Sting ovary risk*
Gustav Holst	*Vast hog slut*
Arnold Schoenberg	*Old bench groaners*

DRAMATISTS

Howard Barker	*Dark whore bar*
Robert Anderson	*Rear snob rodent*
David Campton	*Vacant odd imp*
Alice Childress	*Leech lad crisis*
Sarah Daniels	*Sad alien rash*
Phillip Hayes Dean	*"Hip play" headlines*
Christopher Durang	*Ugh! Hard-core prints*
Barry England	*Balder granny*
David Fennario	*Arid nova fiend*
Richard Foreman	*In hard-core farm*
Samuel Beckett	*Meekest at club*
Trevor Griffiths	*Right stiff rover*
Oliver Hailey	*Eh! I evil royal*
Ron Hutchinson	*In on thrush con*
Stanley Eveling	*Tiny angel elves*
Thomas Kilroy	*I smoky harlot*
Deborah Levy	*Hey! Bad lover*
Frank McGuinness	*Cunning serf mask*
Susan Miller	*Small urines*
Richard Nelson	*Cold inner rash*
Dennis Potter	*Pertinent sod*
Christina Reid	*Irish acne dirt*
Peter Shaffer	*Fresh fat peer*
Stuart Sherman	*Hears tantrums*
Hugh Whitemore	*Huge other whim*

EUROPEAN ARTISTS

Sir Lawrence Alma-Tadema	*Wet as all-American dream*
Albrecht Altdorfer	*Braced for tart hell*
Andrea del Sarto	*So, retarded anal*
Sofonisba Anguissola	*If I snob analogous ass*
Antonello da Messina	*And tonal anomalies*
Jules Bastien-Lepage	*Jesus! A bleeping tale*
Giovanni Bellini	*Inane living boil*
Sandro Botticelli	*Obstetrician doll*
Antonio Canaletto	*Not a neat location*
Antonio Allegri da Correggio	*Oi! Arrogant gorilla genocide!*
Robert Campin	*Nice brat romp*
Leonardo da Vinci	*Vindaloo and rice*
Artemisia Gentileschi	*Imagines earliest itch*
Vincent Van Gogh	*Changing TV oven*
Pieter de Hooch	*The heroic dope*
Angelica Kauffman	*Annual fake magic*
Gustav Klimt	*Vast milk gut*
Ambrogio Lorenzetti	*I'm a rotten booze girl*
Michelangelo Buonarroti	*Machine tooling labourer*
Pablo Picasso	*Boils soap cap*
Hieronymous Bosch	*Boo! He is horny scum*
Raffaello Sanzio Raphael	*A hall oozes far airplane*
Donatello	*Atoll node*
Titian Vecellio	*Vain toilet lice*
Paolo Veronese	*Porno love ease*

FAMOUS PAINTINGS

The Adoration Of the Magi	*Hoho! I am a rotating defeat*
Mona Lisa	*I also man*
St Peter Healing With His Shadow	*Worthwhile high-speed Satanist*
St Francis Preaches To The Birds	*First-rate archbishop's descent*
The Scream	*Rat scheme*
Night Cafe	*Fight acne*
St George And The Dragon	*Danger! Gonads together*
Birth Of Venus	*Five-ton brush*
Old Man With His Grandson	*This dog now in marshland*
Susanna Bathing	*Thugs in bananas*
The Last Supper	*The slut papers*
The Dead Christ	*Ditched haters*
Portrait Of A Woman	*Now I am a tart proof*
The Crucifixion	*Toxic ruin chief*
The Descent From The Cross	*Stretched sheet conforms*
The Creation Of Adam	*O man! Erotic fathead*
Christina's World	*I scorn wild trash*
Autumn Leaves	*Am avenue slut*
The Scapegoat	*Gestapo cheat*
Moulin de la Galette	*Ultimate golden ale*
In The Orchestra Pit	*Rich rotten ape shit*
Portrait Of Malisse	*Sorriest Mafia plot*
Fight In The Arcade	*Hate arch-fiend git*
The Persistence Of Memory	*Smoothest creepy firemen*
The Painter's Studio	*Hated superstition*

PANTOMIMES AND PANTO CHARACTERS

Aladdin and His Magic Lamp	*Sad aching ill-paid mad man*
Wicked Uncle Abanazar	*Unbalance cake wizard*
Ali Baba and the Forty Thieves	*Ha! Bovinely battier fatheads*
Babes In The Wood	*Boo bawdiest hen*
Baron Hardup	*Had a porn rub*
Puss In Boots	*I snoop busts*
Beauty and the Beast	*Abuse that bad teeny*
Cinderella and the Glass Slipper	*Snarling apeshit declared spell*
Demon King	*Kind gnome*
Dick Whittington	*Kid not twitching*
Snow White and the Seven Dwarves	*Few withdrawn heaven-sent sods*
The Sleeping Beauty	*yeah, use bent piglet!*
Mother Goose	*Some hot ogre*
Hansel and Gretel	*Hell! Satan gender*
The Golden Goose	*Eh? Good snot glee*
Goldilocks and the Three Bears	*Hoho! Drudge blackest latrines*
Fairy Godmother	*Oh my God! Fart hire*
Humpty-Dumpty	*Myth pump duty*
The Rat King	*Hating trek*
Little Jack Horner	*Jerk latrine cloth*
Little Miss Muffet	*Misfit slut felt me*
Little Red Riding Hood	*The drooling idle dirt*
Sinbad The Sailor	*Isn't airhead slob*
Pied Piper of Hamelin	*Pale if pimped heroin*
Prince Charming	*Enriching cramp*

POEMS

The Lady Of Shalot	*Oh, floats deathly*
Ode To A Nightingale	*Genitalia on the dog*
The Highwayman	*Aha! Whinge myth*
Stop All The Clocks	*Lack splotches lot*
How Do I Love Thee	*Oh! The viewed loo*
Upon Westminster Bridge	*Determins grown-up bits*
The Owl And The Pussycat	*Hated slushy twat ponce*
Anthem For Doomed Youth	*Lust watched pantyhose*
Everyone Sang	*A nosy revenge*
Dover Beach	*Breed havoc*
The Listeners	*The stern lies*
The Soldier	*Dire hotels*
When You Are Old	*Ahoy! Lower nude*
The Great Lover	*Revert hog tale*
The Ruined Male	*The idle manure*
A Red, Red Rose	*Deers roared*
The Hound Of Heaven	*Ho ho! Even hated fun!*
The Passionate Shepherd	*Parentheses hide pathos*
Naming Of Parts	*Poignant farms*
Jenny Kissed Me	*I'm Jensen's dyke*
Warming Her Pearls	*Seraphim wrangler*
Love's Philosophy	*Shh! Evil soppy loo*
She Walks In Beauty	*Blue-white yank ass*
Diary Of A Church Mouse	*Ahoy! Heroic fraud scum*
Prayer Before Birth	*Probe hefty barrier*

POETS

Geoffrey Chaucer	*Hey! Cure frogface!*
Sir Thomas Wyatt	*Atom was thirsty*
Edmund Spenser	*Mend suspender*
Thomas Gray	*O my hag's rat!*
Sir John Betjeman	*Man jeers thin job*
Henry Vaughan	*A hungry haven*
Alexander Pope	*Paean explored*
William Blake	*I make bill law*
Robert Burns	*Snort rubber*
William Wordsworth	*Whom worst wild liar*
Mr John Keats	*Month as jerk*
Samuel Taylor Coleridge	*Small creature ideology*
Christina Rossetti	*Isn't rash eroticist*
Alfred, Lord Tennyson	*Slanderer, not fondly*
Robert Browning	*Grrr! Went in boob*
Elizabeth Barrett Browning	*Brewing the zanier blob tart*
Gerard Manley Hopkins	*My long-haired spanker*
Seamus Heaney	*See — easy human*
Matthew Arnold	*Damn wet harlot*
Percy Bysshe Shelley	*Hey! Bless shyly creep*
George Gordon Noel	*No! Golden ogre gore*
Mister John Dryden	*Red horny jest mind*
George Herbert	*Hog beer regret*
Andrew Marvell	*Mr lavender law*
William Butler Yeats	*A writable limey slut*

SHAKESPEARE'S WORKS AND CHARACTERS

The Two Gentlemen Of Verona	*He now forgotten lame event*
Richard Duke Of York	*Did fake yuck horror*
Titus Andronicus	*Unionist custard*
Venus And Adonis	*Deans sound vain*
Love's Labour Lost	*Lout's overall boss*
A Midsummer Night's Dream	*Harmed mad smug minister*
Romeo And Juliet	*Injured loo mate*
Friar Lawrence	*Fine rear crawl*
John Of Gaunt	*Na! Hot fun jog*
Much Ado About Nothing	*Ouch! Bought damnation*
Julius Caesar	*A! Us curse jail*
Othello	*O! To Hell!*
Troilus And Cressida	*Darn! Suicidal tosser*
Measure For Measure	*A museum or free arse?*
All's Well That Ends Well	*Hell! Let's slant lewd law*
Timon Of Athens	*Not of mean hits*
The History Of King Lear	*Angriest filthy hooker*
The Tragedy Of Macbeth	*Crafty behemoth gated*
Antony And Cleopatra	*Actor annoyed a plant*
Pericles, Prince Of Tyre	*Creepy cretin profiles*
The Winter's Tale	*The latrineís wet*
Sebastian	*Na! Is beast*
Prospero, Duke of Milan	*O dear me! foul porn skip*
The Two Noble Kinsmen	*Whom ennobles kitten?*
Lady Macbeth	*My! Bald cheat!*

THEATRES AND ENTERTAINMENT VENUES

The Victoria Apollo	*Alcohol poet trivia*
Barbican Concert Hall	*Anarchic central blob*
Albany Empire	*Preen amiably*
Donmar Warehouse	*Oh dear! Woman user*
Victoria Palace Theatre	*Vicar pale at erotic heat*
The Royal Albert Hall	*Really a brothel halt*
Royal Festival Hall	*Fails lavatory hell*
Dockland's Arena	*Naked carnal sod*
The Palladium	*Dial up Hamlet*
The Theatre Royal Haymarket	*Hey, meek hate a harlotry tart*
London Hippodrome	*Oh no! porn imploded*
Manchester Apollo	*Clapton reams hole*
Adelphi Theatre	*Leatherhead pit*
London Coliseum	*Clone loo nudism*
Royal Opera House	*Hey! Poor soul area*
Prince of Wale's Theatre	*Woe, parenthetical serf*
Duke of York Theatre, London	*Try Toledo naked hooker fun*
Drury Lane, Theatre Royal	*Adultery ran there*
The Young Vic	*Ugh! city oven*
Ulster Hall, Belfast	*Flares halt bullets*
Waterfront Hall, Belfast	*Brothel staff learnt law*
Royal Ballet Theatre	*Tart really beat hole*
Birmingham NEC	*Grim main bench*
Glasgow NECC	*Gang close WC*
Her Majesty's Theatre	*Jet-setter's hay harem*
Wyndhams Theatre	*Trashy when mated*

AMERICAN COMEDIES OF THE 1960S AND 1970S

The Addams Family	*My dismal fathead*
The Adventures of Ozzie And Harriet	*Nine-to-five Zarathustra dozed here*
My Favourite Martian	*Motivate unfair army*
All In The Family	*Finally the mail*
The Andy Griffith Show	*Iffy hawthorn sighted*
Bachelor Father	*Ha! Brothel farce*
The Munsters	*Mesh nutters*
The Beverly Hillbillies	*Slithery evil bible hell*
Bewitched	*Bitch weed*
The Brady Bunch	*Hey! And hurt BBC!*
The Dick Van Dyke Show	*Envy whacked hot kids*
Happy Days	*Had spy pay*
The Flintstones	*Ton's tense filth*
The Ghost And Mrs Muir	*I'm thunderstorm shag*
Gilligan's Island	*Dialling sin lags*
Green Acres	*Screen rage*
Hogan's Heroes	*Shag one horse*
I Dream Of Jeannie	*A fine jeer domain*
Laverne And Shirley	*Hardly venereal sin*
Mister Ed	*Demerits*
Mork And Mindy	*My! Mad on drink!*
The Partridge Family	*Tried filthy rampage*
Rowan And Martin's Laugh In	*Warlord's an inhuman giant*
Welcome Back Kotter	*Make clocktower bet*
The WRKP In Cincinnati Show	*China township tick winner*

AMERICAN COMEDIES OF THE 1980S AND 1990S

Beavis And Butthead	*Bathtub's naive dead*
South Park	*OK, Up trash!*
Caroline In The City	*I crotchety in alien*
The Cosby Show	*Shh! Cowboy set*
Designing Women	*Widening gnomes*
Diff'rent Strokes	*Deft for stinkers*
Doogie Howser MD	*Gosh! Weirdo mode*
Family Ties	*Is fat limey*
The Fresh Prince Of Bel Air	*Oh, reprehensible traffic*
The Golden Girls	*Still hog gender*
Grace Under Fire	*Fine career drug*
Harry And The Hendersons	*Darn! Harshest horny need!*
Home Improvement	*Oh, I'm temper venom*
Kate And Allie	*Like a neat lad*
King Of The Hill	*Liken hog filth*
The Larry Sanders Show	*Rewards thorny hassle*
Married With Children	*Wed her third criminal*
Moonlighting	*Glinting homo*
Ren And Stimpy	*Empty innards*
Sledge Hammer	*She rammed leg*
The Simpsons	*Shine stomps*
Saturday Night Live	*Huge ratty invalids*
The Tracey Ullman Show	*Unseemly harlot watch*
The Wonder Years	*Worthy serenade*
Night Court	*Gothic runt*

AMERICAN TELEVISION ACTORS

Kevin Sorbo	*Is over bonk*
George Clooney	*Cool energy ego*
Matthew Perry	*Empty her wart*
David Schwimmer	*Craved dim whims*
Matt Le Blanc	*Men ball tact*
Noah Wyle	*Low hyena*
John Lithgow	*Thin hog jowl*
Nicholas Lea	*I clash alone*
Joseph Gordon Levitt	*Overnight dope jolts*
French Stewart	*Fawn stretcher*
Rick Schroder	*Rich red rocks*
Dylan McDermott	*Mr. Mottled Candy*
Anthony Edwards	*Nasty and whored*
Eriq La Salle	*Sell Iraq ale*
Mitch Peleggi	*Gel might epic*
Kelsey Grammer	*Meek merry slag*
David Hyde Pierce	*Dire hyped advice*
Sammo Hung	*Hansom mug*
Scott Bakula	*Lout sat back*
Dean Stockwell	*Stale lewd conk*
Jerry Seinfield	*Friendly jeers*
Kyle McLachlan	*Calm lanky lech*
Gary Cole	*Clay ogre*
Ted Danson	*Nest on dad*
Patrick Duffy	*"Fifty Duck" rap*

American Television Actresses

Gillian Anderson	*No aliens, darling*
Calista Flockhart	*LA chick rafts a lot*
Kirstie Alley	*Satire likely*
Sara Michelle Gellar	*A sheer male call girl*
Stephanie Beacham	*A sheep, a mean bitch*
Courtney Cox	*Ex-con outcry*
Jennifer Aniston	*Fan in joint sneer*
Kristen Johnson	*No! Thin jerk sons*
Julianna Margulies	*Injure small iguana*
Gloria Reuben	*An uglier bore*
Kellie Martin	*I'm neat killer*
Brooke Shields	*Heroes' slob kid*
Lisa Kudrow	*O! Kid walrus*
Pamela Anderson Lee	*Real lemonade panel*
Jobeth Williams	*Him bestial jowl*
Jennifer Love Hewitt	*Invert fine hot jewel*
Miss Neve Campbell	*Even climbs maples*
Star Joan Collins	*Join Satan scroll*
Roseanne Barr	*Near rear snob*
Kim Delaney	*Menial dyke*
Tori Spelling	*Isn't pole-girl*
Terry Hatcher	*He cherry tart*
Shannen Doherty	*Randy honest hen*
Sharon Lawrence	*Now sheer carnal*
Farrah Fawcett	*Fat farce wrath*

BBC SPORTS PRESENTERS

Barry Davies	*Bravery aids*
Mister John Motson	*Oh! Men joint storms*
Tony Gubba	*Botany bug*
Mister Jon Champion	*Oh man! I'm sin project*
Clive Everton	*Encore! Evil TV*
David Vine	*Vivid dean*
Peter O'Sullevan	*Pale volunteers*
Richard Pitman	*Rancid pit harm*
Ray French	*Cherry fan*
Jim Neilly	*Mini jelly*
Murray Walker	*Murky rear law*
David Coleman	*Acid lad venom*
Stuart Storey	*Sure tart toys*
Brendan Foster	*Brand softener*
Paul Dickenson	*Nice loud spank*
Bill McLaren	*Mr libel clan*
Nigel Starmer Smith	*Shelter immigrants*
Rob Andrew	*Drab owner*
Peter Alliss	*Stale perils*
Mister Alex Hay	*A slithery exam*
Peter Scudamore	*Mare prosecuted*
Richie Benaud	*I in rude beach*
Tony Lewis	*Wino style*
Sue Barker	*Sure break*
Steve Rider	*Severe dirt*

BRITISH SOAP OPERA CHARACTERS AND ACTORS

Mandy Dingle	*Mending lady*
Butch Dingle	*Dunce blight*
Jackie Corkhill	*Kill, heroic Jack!*
Mister Jimmy Corkhill	*Kill a chic joker*
Dean Sullivan	*Annual devils*
Beth Jordache	*Eh! Hard object*
Terry Sullivan	*Slurry evil ant*
Seth Armstrong	*Trash germ snot*
Stan Richards	*Crass rat hind*
Betty Eagleton	*Beat gentle toy*
Paula Tilbrook	*Park a lout boil*
Jacqueline Pirie	*In queer jail epic*
Rachel Hughes	*Huge lech rash*
Eric Pollard	*Replica lord*
Christopher Chittel	*The rich let chips rot*
Jack Sugden	*Suck jag end*
Clive Hornby	*Inch by lover*
Chris Tate	*The racist*
Melandra Burrows	*Brawn rude morals*
Claire King	*Raking lice*
Alan Turner	*Neural rant*
Richard Thorp	*Hard rich poet*
Scott Windsor	*Isn't worst cad*
Viv Windsor	*Vivid 'n rows*
Sarah Sugden	*Darn! Huge ass!*

BRITISH TV COMEDIES OF THE 1960S & 1970S

All Gas And Gaiters	*Genial as Gladstone*
The Army Game	*Ahem! Gay term*
Are You Being Served	*Greedy envious bear*
Rising Damp	*Is grim pad*
Bless This House	*Blue host hisses*
Carry On Laughing	*Ouch! An angry girl!*
Oh Brother!	*Hero throb*
Some Mothers Do 'Ave 'Em	*Move home-made tosser*
Dave Allen At Large	*Revealed a gallant*
Doctor In The House	*Hot seduction hero*
The Fall And Rise Of Reginald Perrin	*Profile a Neanderthal girlfriend*
Father Dear Father	*Ha! 'Freed raft' hater*
Fawlty Towers	*Two felt as wry*
Steptoe And Son	*Teased non-stop*
George And Mildred	*Old deranged grime*
The Good Life	*Heed loo gift*
It Ain't Half Hot Mum	*Oh! I am mutant filth*
The Kenny Everett Video Show	*Hottest whenever I've dyke on*
Last Of The Summer Wine	*I'm somewhat resentful*
The Likely Lads	*Hell! Dyke's tail!*
Man About The House	*Ah, beauteous month*
Love Thy Neighbour	*Ugh! Horny lovebite*
The Morecambe And Wise Show	*Him beheads worm-eaten cows*
Monty Python's Flying Circus	*Comfortingly sunny itch spy*
Going Straight	*Tights in aggro*

BRITISH TV COMEDIES OF THE 1980S & 1990S

Black Adder The Second	*Deathbed cock slander*
The Brittas Empire	*Him prettier beast*
Carrott's Lib	*Broils tract*
The Comic Strip Presents...	*Cheers! Impotent scripts*
The Young Ones	*Hey! No tongues!*
Drop The Dead Donkey	*Key Don threaded pod*
Father Ted	*Deft Earth*
Have I Got News For You	*Heavens! Our goofy wit*
Girls On Top	*Groin plots*
Goodnight Sweetheart	*Oh no! Egghead twitters*
Jeeves And Wooster	*'Vote now!' Ass jeered*
Keeping Up Appearances	*Keep papering saucepan*
Shooting Stars	*It's hosts groan*
The Mary Whitehouse Experience	*Ho hum! Three piece sewer anxiety*
Men Behaving Badly	*'Gamble behind navy*
The Mrs Merton Show	*Hmm! Threw on tosser*
The New Statesman	*That wet meanness*
Not The Nine O'Clock News	*Now let's choke innocent*
One Foot In the Grave	*Ho! Often over-eating*
Only Fools And Horses	*No! Sod loony flashers*
Rab C. Nesbitt	*Bent sic brat*
Vic Reeves Big Night Out	*Voice cubverting eight*
Spitting Image	*I emitting gasp*
Auf Wiedersehen Pet	*Featured sheep wine*
The Bottle Boys	*O! the testy blob*

CARTOON CHARACTERS

Mickey Mouse	*Oi! seem mucky*
Minnie Mouse	*I'm noise menu*
Betty Boop	*Byte to bop*
Fred Flintstone	*Daft Lenin frost*
Pluto The Dog	*Potted ghoul*
Simba The Lion	*Inhabits mole*
Grumpy The Dwarf	*Ugh! Fry mad twerp*
Lisa Simpson	*Slim passion*
Dopey The Dwarf	*Weepy dad froth*
Maggie Simpson	*Me imposing gas*
Barney Rubble	*Yearn blubber*
Porky The Pig	*Kept hip orgy*
Sylvester The Cat	*TV lechery states*
Tweetie Pie	*I petite ewe*
Topcat	*Tap cot*
Jerry The Mouse	*Yum! Jester hero*
Yogi Bear	*Bogey air*
Scooby Doo	*Boo! Coy sod*
Scrappy Doo	*Parody cops*
Inspector Gadget	*Gasping detector*
Hero Johnny Bravo	*Horny van job*
Dick Dastardly	*Did acts darkly*
Marvin The Martian	*Vain tit man harmer*
Bart Simpson	*Armpit snobs*
Homer Simpson	*Morphine moss*

CHILDREN'S TV SHOWS

Camberwick Green	*Be grim acne wreck*
Captain Pugwash	*Await punch gasp*
Captain Scarlet	*Rascal pittance*
The Clangers	*Large stench*
Danger Mouse	*Demons argue*
The Flinstones	*Seen snot filth*
Dogtanian	*Tango and I*
Rainbow	*Wino bar*
The Flowerpot Men	*Nephew felt motor*
The Teletubbies	*Beetles hit tube*
Grange Hill	*Her ill gang*
Hector's House	*Ouch! He tosser*
Bagpuss	*Pub sags*
The Wombles	*Bestow helm*
Power Rangers	*Gropes warren*
The Magic Roundabout	*Thou doubting camera*
Pinky And Perky	*Kinky red nappy*
Muffin The Mule	*Eh! Mute film fun*
Roobarb And Custard	*Drab absurd cartoon*
Scooby Doo, Where Are You?	*O dear! You cowboy heroes*
Skippy The Bush Kangaroo	*Kinky photographs abuse*
Stingray	*Tiny rags*
Sweet Valley High	*Hell! The gay wives*
Sabrina The Teenage Witch	*The satanic whinge beater*
Teenage Mutant Hero Turtles	*Ensure huge total treatment*

CORONATION STREET CHARACTERS & ACTORS

Julie Goodyear	*Glue joy roadie*
Deirdre Barlow	*Idler wardrobe*
Vera Duckworth	*Ha! Crude TV work*
Ken Barlow	*Boner walk*
Audrey Roberts	*So dreary brute*
Sally Webster	*Stall by sewer*
Kevin Webster	*Brew eve stink*
Steve McDonald	*Mad TV enclosed*
Emily Bishop	*Blimey! I posh!*
Mister Jim McDonald	*Scrammed mild joint*
Hilda Ogden	*An idled hog*
Roy Barraclough	*A gay club horror*
Alec Gilroy	*A glory lice*
Sue Nicholls	*Hell's cousin*
William Tarney	*I'm literal yawn*
Mavis Wilton	*Low Vitamins*
Curly Watts	*Wry slut act*
Rita Fairclough	*Foul tragic hair*
Percy Sugden	*Creepy dungs*
Phyllis Pearce	*Slippery leach*
Alma Baldwin	*I am bland law*
Alma Sedgewick	*Wicked lame gas*
Michael Baldwin	*I'm bad winkle*
Martin Platt	*Rampant tilt*
Kevin Kennedy	*Even kinky den*

CULT TV SHOWS

Twin Peaks	*Pink waste*
Thirtysomething	*Shy nighttime rot*
Doctor Who	*Torchwood*
Kolchak The Night Stalker	*Thank legs, kick the harlot*
Eerie, Indiana	*Inane idea ire*
The Professionals	*Fine harlot's poses*
Charlie's Angels	*Slashing cereal*
The Fugitive	*Eh! I've fit gut*
Man In A Suitcase	*Its manic nausea*
Mission Impossible	*I'm semi-poison bliss*
Perry Mason	*Ransom prey*
The Protectors	*The rotter cops*
The Saint	*Hesitant*
The Untouchables	*Hot unsubtle ache*
Alias Smith And Jones	*Joins the sad animals*
Davy Crockett	*Cocky TV trade*
Hopalong Cassidy	*Diagonal psychos*
Little House On The Prairie	*Lethal repetitious heroin*
The Waltons	*Stealth won*
The Lone Ranger	*Hero entangler*
The Wild Wild West	*Lewd whistled wit*
Robin Of Sherwood	*Soon forbid whore*
Prisoner Cell Block H	*Scorch libel plonker*
Peyton Place	*Pale potency*
Northern Exposure	*Sure! Next porn hero*

EASTENDERS CHARACTERS & ACTORS

Pauline Fowler	*Powerful alien*
Michelle Fowler	*I'm fellow lecher*
Grant Mitchell	*Ten girl match*
Matthew Rose	*He's a two-term*
Steve McFadden	*TV fame descend*
Bianca Butcher	*Bacteria bunch*
Patsy Palmer	*Masterly pap*
Robbie Jackson	*Basic born joke*
Arthur Fowler	*Her artful row*
Steve Owen	*We see on TV*
Carol Jackson	*Jackal's croon*
Daniela Denby-Ashe	*Yeah, bad and senile!*
Pat Butcher	*Brute patch*
Frank Butcher	*Bunch trek far*
Martine McCutcheon	*To crunch mincemeat*
Wendy Richards	*Sandwich dryer*
Gillian Taylforth	*Flight rationally*
Leslie Grantham	*Hell! I am strange*
Anita Dobson	*Not a snob aid*
Letitia Dean	*Entail a diet*
Martin Fowler	*Wart life norm*
Barbara Windsor	*Raw or bad brains*
Teresa Di Marco	*Atomic readers*
Simon Wicks	*I'm sick cows*
Beppe di Marco	*I'm a bed copper*
Tiffany Mitchell	*Felt filthy manic*

FEMALE TELEVISION PRESENTERS

Miss Jill Dando	*Minds old jails*
Cheryl Baker	*Lechery bark*
Floella Benjamin	*Menial fallen job*
Gaby Roslin	*Grainy slob*
Lorraine Kelly	*Killer on early*
Anne Diamond	*Inane odd man*
Carole Smilie	*Slice mole liar*
Sarah Greene	*Rehearse nag*
Susannah Charlton	*Nonchalant as rush*
Gail Porter	*Grope trial*
Gloria Hunniford	*Hard in foul groin*
Maggie Philbin	*Hi! Pig blame gin*
Jennifer Powell	*Elfin porn jewel*
Denise Van Outen	*Insane nude vote*
Esther Rantzen	*Stern rent haze*
Anneka Rice	*Inane creak*
Johanna Hargreaves	*Rang Jehova's arena*
Anne Robinson	*No! Born insane!*
Valerie Singleton	*Resignation level*
Janet Street Porter	*Re-arrest potent jet*
Carol Vorderman	*Damn vocal error*
Cilla Black	*A ball click*
Katie Puckrick	*I kick up racket*
Emma Forbes	*Fame robs me*
Debbie Greenwood	*Wed boogie bender*

HOME & AWAY CHARACTERS & ACTORS

Kate Richie	*Hire ace kit*
Belinda Emmett	*Bed-time lament*
Rebecca Nash	*Bare chances*
Nic Testoni	*Notices ITN*
Travis Nash	*Harass in TV*
Mister Ryan Clark	*Scary Kremlin rat*
Rebecca Cartwright	*Big rat-catcher crew*
Ray Meagher	*Hear my rage*
Alf Stewart	*Was flatter*
Irene Roberts	*Reinsert robe*
Ailsa Stewart	*Astarte wails*
Donald Fisher	*Fondled hairs*
Norman Coburn	*Can burn moron*
Marilyn Fisher	*Irishman flyer*
Emily Symons	*My nosy slime*
Kristy Wright	*Grr! Kitty wish*
Duncan Stewart	*Wasn't dunce rat*
Ryan Kwanten	*New yank rant*
Bree Desborough	*Debug sober hero*
David Woodley	*View lady dodo*
Antoinette Byron	*Nonentity boater*
Kimberley Cooper	*Bore mockery pile*
Zac Drayson	*Na! Crazy sod*
Graeme Squires	*Requires games*
Ben Unwin	*Nun in web*

MALE TELEVISION PRESENTERS

Michael Aspel	*Is ample leach*
Mister Jeremy Paxman	*Remains jammy expert*
Jeremy Beadle	*Jeered by male*
David Bellamy	*Evil mad baldy*
Gyles Brandreth	*Held by stranger*
Neil Buchanan	*An alien bunch*
Gordon Burns	*Born on drugs*
Jonathan Ross	*Has no snot jar*
Nick Ross	*Rock sins*
Keith Chegwin	*Hit geek winch*
Andy Crane	*Randy acne*
Phillip Schofield	*Childish life plop*
Noel Edmonds	*Mended loons*
Sir Robin Day	*Is randy biro*
David Dimblebey	*My! I bed bad devil*
Bruce Forsyth	*Frosty cherub*
Sir David Frost	*Sordid TV fairs*
Denis Norden	*Send in drone*
Bob Holness	*He snob slob*
Richard Whiteley	*Hi! Wild treachery*
Desmond Lyman	*Damn sly demon*
Richard Madeley	*Mild dreary ache*
Magnus Magnusson	*Summon anus gangs*
Richard O'Brien	*Nice horrid bar*
Michael Parkinson	*Shrink a policeman*

NEIGHBOURS CHARACTERS & ACTORS

Madge Bishop	*I'm bog shaped*
Anne Charleston	*Enchants a loner*
Harold Bishop	*Ho ho! Drab lips*
Helen Daniels	*Handle senile*
Charlene Robinson	*No bachelor sinner*
Scott Robinson	*Croon stint - sob*
Jim Robinson	*Minor job sin*
Paul Robinson	*No labour spin*
Stefan Dennis	*Dense infants*
Melanie Pearson	*Mean alien poser*
Mark Little	*Me kill tart*
Guy Pearce	*Pure cagey*
Ian Smith	*Main hits*
Kristian Schmid	*It kind christmas*
Mrs Mangel	*Me Mr. Slang*
Todd Landers	*Trodden lads*
Lucy Robinson	*Burn sic loony*
Lou Carpenter	*A porn lecture*
Tom Oliver	*Evil motor*
Annalise Hartman	*Saner than animal*
Kimberley Davies	*Dim yak believers*
Lucinda Cowden	*Nude acid clown*
Scott Michaelson	*Hot manic closest*
Kyle Maclaughlin	*Chalky glum alien*
Danni Stark	*Satan drink*

SCI-FI & FANTASY TV SHOWS OF THE 1960S & 1970S

The Adventures Of Superman	*Tape adventurous freshmen*
The Avengers	*Revenge hats*
Batman And Robin	*Main nob and brat*
The Time Tunnel	*Teeth lint menu*
The Champions	*I'm honest chap*
The Incredible Hulk	*Hell! Nuke dire bitch*
The Invaders	*Envied trash*
The Original Star Trek	*Irritant harlot geeks*
The Invisible Man	*Inhabits evil men*
Land Of The Giants	*Total gnash fiend*
Lost In Space	*Snot special*
Man From Atlantis	*O man! Tartan films*
The Man From Uncle	*Foul merchant men*
Men Into Space	*Nice moan pest*
Mork And Mindy	*My! Mad on drink*
My Favourite Martian	*Immature faint ovary*
Out Of The Unknown	*Thou onto new funk*
The Outer Limits	*Loutish termite*
The Prisoner	*The porn rise*
Space Patrol	*Strop palace*
The Twilight Zone	*Zenith hotel twig*
Phoenix Five	*Fine pox hive*
Planet Of The Apes	*False potent heap*
The Secret Service	*Sever erect ethics*
The Six Million Dollar Man	*Hello! Instil Marxian mold*

SCI FI & FANTASY TV SHOWS OF THE 1980S & 1990S

V The Miniseries	*I'm in severe shit*
The Amazing Spiderman	*Parenthesizing madam*
The X Files	*Hex itself*
Quantum Leap	*Equal map nut*
Star Trek The Next Generation	*Inaner rotten trash geek text*
Star Trek Voyager	*Streaky grave rot*
Battlestar Gallactica	*Blast it! Legal contract*
Buck Rogers	*Borg sucker*
Children Of The Dogstar	*Fetched drooling trash*
Babylon Five	*Bible of navy*
Edge Of Darkness	*Dense freak gods*
Hitch Hiker's Guide To The Galaxy	*Heigh-ho! Sated trickily huge tax*
Terrahawks	*Trash wreak*
The Return Of Captain Nemo	*Ahem! Penetrator function*
Superboy	*Rosy pube*
The Tripods	*Dope thirst*
The New Adventures Of Superman	*Penetrates unwashed fur venom*
American Gothic	*Imagine a crotch*
Millennium	*In null mime*
Wonder Woman	*Now raw demon*
Sapphire And Steel	*Plead parenthesis*
Knight Rider	*Her dirt king*
Alien Nation	*Inane ant oil*
Deep Space Nine	*Dense acne pipe*
Space Precinct	*PC antics creep*

STAR TREK ACTORS AND CHARACTERS

William Shatner	*Well I am in trash*
Leonard Nimoy	*Dire loony man*
Patrick Stewart	*Trackers trap wit*
Nichelle Nichols	*Oh hell! In clinches*
Walter Koenig	*Tweaking role*
DeForrest Kelly	*Foretell red sky*
George Takei	*Oi! Great geek*
James Doohan	*Ha! jeans doom*
Grace Lee Whitney	*Lay eighteen crew*
Captain James T. Kirk	*A armpit skin jacket*
Ensign Pavel Chekov	*Have sloven pecking*
Lieutenant Uhura	*Untrue! A alien hut!*
Doctor Leonard McCoy	*Moody cold cancer rot*
The Vulcan Spock	*Clean up shock TV*
Marina Surtis	*I'm a star's ruin*
Deanna Troi	*Radiant one*
Beverly Crusher	*Curb her severely*
Jonathan Frakes	*Hosanna! Fat jerk*
Commander William Riker	*Menial warlord mimicker*
Wil Wheaton	*Wino wealth*
Wesley Crusher	*Hey! Screw rules!*
John de Lancie	*He conned jail*
Michelle Forbes	*Bore leech films*
Commander Data	*Act! Drama demon*
Captain Jean-Luc Picard	*Japan circulated panic*

TELEVISION COP SHOWS

Yellow Thread Street	*Deletes wet harlotry*
The Untouchables	*Ouch! Beneath slut*
The Streets Of San Francisco	*Coherent Satanist scoffers*
Starsky And Hutch	*Hard tasty chunks*
Juliet Bravo	*Jovial brute*
Jake And The Fatman	*Then the anti-thief hog*
Sledge Hammer	*Male germ shed*
The Ruth Rendall Mysteries	*It's the nasty murderer hell*
Rockcliffe's Babies	*Bribes off slick ace*
The Rockford Files	*Fostered rich folk*
Return Of The Saint	*Fine southern tart*
Hill Street Blues	*Belt sterile lush*
The Protectors	*Hotter cop rest*
Police Woman	*I'm a low ponce*
A Man Called Ironside	*No! Is declared animal*
The New Adventures Of Perry Mason	*Renowned myth of perverts nausea*
The Nancy Drew Mysteries	*Hey! Screwy determinants*
Naked City	*Cat kidney*
Murder She Wrote	*Rude whore's term*
Moonlighting	*Hinting gloom*
The Mod Squad	*Doh! Mad quest*
Midnight Caller	*Hell! Tragic mind*
Mancuso FBI	*A bin of scum*
Highway Patrol	*A holy pig wrath*
Man With A Suitcase	*What? I sauciest man*

TV DETECTIVES OF THE 1960S & 1970S

Piot Van der Valk	*Viler vodka pant*
Detective Jack Regan	*Ejected tragic knave*
George Carter	*Erect ogre rag*
Mike Stone	*Is not meek*
Steve Keller	*Lest elk veer*
Dave Starsky	*Very sad task*
Ken Hutchinson	*No ethnic hunks*
Charlie Barlow	*A horrible claw*
Barnaby Jones	*Enjoys bra ban*
Simon Templar	*Mop terminals*
Sabrina Duncan	*Crud in bananas*
Detective Kelly Garret	*Cleverly edit geek tart*
Marty Hopkirk	*Try khaki romp*
Captain Amos Burke	*OK maniac rat pubes*
Suzanne Anderson	*Earns a dozen nuns*
Tony Petrocelli	*Pretty loon lice*
Perry Mason	*Manor preys*
Robert Ironside	*Dire rioter snob*
Chief Inspector Maignet	*Cheating imperfections*
Lt. Theo Kojak	*Hot joke talk*
Jason King	*Sank jingo*
Dan Matthews	*Attends Wham*
James Hazell, investigator	*Evil harlot's magazine jest*
Steve McGarrett	*Erect tar's TV gem*
The Green Hornet	*Rent the ogre hen*

TV DETECTIVES OF THE 1980S & 1990S

Special Agent Fox Mulder	*X-rated female couplings*
Special Agent Dana Scully	*Satanically plunged case*
Special Agent Dale Cooper	*Slapped ego acceleration*
Harry S. Truman	*Run trash army*
Sergeant TJ Hooker	*Oh no! Greatest jerk*
Inspector Taggart	*Strategic rat pong*
Inspector Wexford	*Crowned sex profit*
Remington Steele	*Resenting omelet*
Jessica Fletcher	*Reject chief lass*
Madie Hayes	*Ha! I am seedy*
David Addison	*Odd sin via dad*
Miss Marple	*Rimless map*
Jack Killian	*Lack jail kin*
Mike Hammer	*Hmm! Meek IRA*
Ricardo Tubbs	*Bit bad cursor*
Sonny Crockett	*Stern not cocky*
Matt Houston	*Shoot mutant*
Nick Mancuso	*Ask comic nun*
Thomas Magnum	*Shotgun mamma*
Jean Darblay	*Lady earn jab*
Jemima Shore	*Is Joe Hammer*
Adam Dagliesh	*Ideal mad shag*
Inspector Morse	*Nice tosser romp*
Christine Cagney	*Nice hysteric nag*
Mary Beth Lacey	*My! A lechery bat*

NEWS AND WEATHER PRESENTERS

Michael Brunson	*Na! Him cruel snob*
Sir Alastair Burnet	*Librarian uses tart*
Sue Carpenter	*Nature's creep*
Mister John Craven	*Venom cretin rash*
Miss Anna Ford	*Finds a ransom*
Philip Hayton	*In hippy loath*
Martyn Lewis	*New slimy rat*
Trevor McDonald	*Old man record TV*
Peter Sissons	*Nose persists*
Alastair Stewart	*A satire stalwart*
Edward Stourton	*Tortured, now sad*
Mister John Suchet	*Shh! Rejection smut*
Francis Wilson	*Crow final sins*
Nicholas Witchell	*Clean this cow hill*
Fiona Armstrong	*Organs of Martin*
Miss Zeinab Badawi	*Zambia's biased win*
Dermot Murnaghan	*Hmm! Arrogant nude*
Roy Sheppard	*Sad hyper pro*
John Stapleton	*Oh! Jet snot plan*
Kirstie Young	*I risky tongue*
Michael Wilson	*I'm nice, shallow*
Weatherman John Ketley	*Hate the namely jerk now*
Michael Fish	*Shh! I'm facile*
Helen Young	*One ugly hen*
Angela Rippon	*Loaning paper*

U.S. COMEDIANS

Andy Griffith	*Fight if randy*
Billy Crystal	*I'll cry stably*
Dick Van Dyke	*Dead kinky CV*
Ellen Degeneres	*Seen leer legend*
Robin Williams	*I warm billions*
Ray Walstan	*Rant always*
Arte Johnson	*He snot on jar*
Barney Miller	*Bell in my rear*
Mr Steve Allen	*Veteran smell*
Bustor Keaton	*Snot outbreak*
Charlie Chaplin	*Pinch chill area*
Danny Kaye	*Na! Any dyke?*
Stan Laurel	*A tall nurse*
Oliver Hardy	*A horrid levy*
Miss Carroll O'Connor	*I'll croon crass moron*
Mickey Rooney	*Yo! I meek crony*
Mary Tyler Moore	*Early memory rot*
Stand-up star Bill Hicks	*Bland, slick push-artist*
George Wendt	*Get newer dog!*
Mister Jim Carey	*I'm army reject, sir!*
Richard Prior	*Rip horrid car*
Dan Ackroyd	*Dandy croak*
Mister Chevy Chase	*Trashy vice scheme*
John Belushi	*Hush line job*
Whoopi Goldberg	*Oh God! Grip bowel!*